This journal belongs to:

_____

If found, please contact:

_____

Kia Kaha
To your golfing greatness

SCORE BETTER

GOLF JOURNAL

TRACK, ANALYZE AND IMPROVE YOUR GAME

Based on research from the podcast
Making A Club Champion
Actionable Interviews Featuring Elite Coaches and Players In The World Of Golf.

MakingAClubChampion.com

GET IN TOUCH/ORDERS/BE A STOCKIST

MakingAClubChampion@gmail.com

Created by Chris Baker & Shady Curi

SCORE BETTER
Golf Journal
www.MakingAClubChampion.com

Copyright © Making A Club Champion

All rights reserved. Without limiting the rights under copyright reserved above, no part of this publication may be reproduced, stored or introduced into a retrieval system, or transmitted, in any form or by any means (electronic, mechanical, photocopying, recording or otherwise), without the prior written permission of both the copyright owner and the publisher of this book.

"The key to pursuing excellence is to embrace an organic, long-term learning process, and not to live in a shell of static, safe mediocrity. Usually, growth comes at the expense of previous comfort or safety."

- Josh Waitzkin

"If you can't outplay them, outwork them."

- Ben Hogan

"We don't rise to the level of our expectations, we fall to the level of our training."

- Archilochus

The European Tour, Chasing Dreams and Mastery
Forward by Mathew Perry

To me golf is far more enjoyable when I stay in the moment, giving all my attention to the shot at hand. When I play well and review my day, this is the most common theme that arises. To put it simply this is the KEY to me playing pure golf.

I believe this explains why after a break from the game you can come back, play free of thought and play far better than imagined. I'm sure all golfers will have experienced this at some point. The idea of taking no expectations of outcome to the course, to a hole or to a single shot has the biggest outcome to my golf than any other single thing.

You see, golf is quite a simple game. It's just we, as humans tend to completely over complicate it, you progress the ball from one position to the next until it finds the bottom of the hole. Yet we stand on a hole, see a hazard, hear a noise or listen to a bad thought, then WACK. The ball has gone nowhere near where we held those aspirations of it flying a few short seconds earlier.

This handbook is a wonderful way to stick to the process. Take note of the outcomes then apply them to your strategy on the course. After completing the practice session you can quickly see the dispersion of your shots. Now, with this information in hand, you can apply it to your next round.

A target shot of 150 yards may be a well-struck 8 iron. But, how often do you strike it well and get it to your target, let alone online? Are you better off taking a 7 iron and swinging with more control? Does your dispersion get better by taking more club? Use this booklet to fine tune how far your clubs go and in what direction are they missing a target?

Let the outcome influence your next round and experiment. See what happens by giving up expectations that you will hit that 8 iron 150 yards. Take a 7 iron instead; it's a far easier game when we miss our targets pin high than it is from the front bunker or short in the water.

As a Pro, these are the types of decisions we make daily, but we are better equipped to make these because of exercises like this one that provides us with a memory bank full of information in which to draw upon when we are on the course. It is through practice sessions like this that we learn to play to our strengths but within our limitations.

Enjoy your practice, experiment with taking the new information you gather on the course and enjoy playing free from expectations. The smile on your face will say it all.

Best wishes,
Matthew Perry: Episode 5, MakingAClubChampion.com

UPGRADE YOUR GAME

"To think is easy. To act is hard. But the hardest thing in the world is to act in accordance with your thinking."
JOHANN WOLFGANG

This journal will help you with the following:

- Identify your big misses
- Calculate your shot dispersion
- Eliminate your most common mistakes
- Learn how to play to your strengths through numbers
- Identify your weaknesses
- Optimizing Golf performance practice
- Golf practice, Skills development, Performance enhancement

ESTABLISHING A BASE LINE: PERFORMANCE IMPROVEMENT PLAN

"Tomorrow becomes never. No matter how small the task, take the first step now!"
TIM FERRISS

The first step with any golfer is to identify the following:

- Where you are now?
- Where you want to be?
- What needs to be done to help get you there?

By structuring a plan in such a way, your goals can now be achievable.

TAKING ACTION & DEVELOPING THE PLAN

"The tighter you cling to your current identity, the harder it becomes to grow beyond it."
JAMES CLEAR

Step #1 - Complete Six Journal Entries

To establish a baseline of where your game is now, your journal will get you to complete six entries before highlighting a strengths and weaknesses assessment of your game.
This will give you enough data to create actionable steps to help you get to where you need to be.

Step #2 - Complete 80/20 Performance Review

The Pareto Principle, or '80-20 Rule' (among other variant names) is one of the simplest and most powerful management tools on the planet.
Utilizing the data you have collected over your first six entries. Your journal will ask you to complete a performance review based on your strengths and weakness.

This will help you identify what you need to practice in your next session and keep you on track of where you are at. Now lets learn more about the importance of the 80/20 rule and why it will help transform your game.

80/20 Performance Review
Strengths vs Weaknesses

The 80/ 20 Principle asserts that a minority of causes, inputs or effort usually lead to a majority of the results, outputs or rewards. Taken literally, this means that for example 80 percent of what you achieve in your game, comes from 20 percent of the time spent.

The reasons why the 80/20 rule is so important, is that we tend to expect that all causes will have roughly the same significance. When it couldn't be further from the truth. Your game can be greatly improved by using the 80/20 rule. Let's show you how.

What is best to focus on? Do you focus on amplifying your strengths and ignore your weaknesses? Or do you focus on trying to limit the weaknesses into less damaging shots and keep the strengths where they are?

The answer depends on which shots are the strengths and which shots are the weaknesses. We always want to get the strengths stronger because they are probably the ones that have got you into the current position to start with, but we also want to limit the weaknesses.

The crucial thing is to find out when you are competing which skill sets you are using the most and try to get those as strong as possible.

E.g. If a player is very good at distance between 100-125 yards into the green, and their proximity to the hole is very strong; but they're not very good from 150-175 yards and when they're competing this is the distance they tend to be challenged with the most and is also the distance they tend to hit in to the green.

Then we want to try and get this as strong as possible because that is the skill that is going to help them the most in reducing their scoring average as quickly as possible.

Using your journal and collecting data on your game, we can highlight your strengths and weaknesses by looking at the "proximity to hole" data you have recorded.

Like the example below. Go through your rounds using the 80/20 principle to highlight what needs to be worked on and what you can make even better.

> Which 20% of my yardages are resulting in 80% of my **DISPERSION** from the hole?
>
> Which 20% of my yardages are resulting in 80% of my **PROXIMITY** to the hole?

Once you have highlighted and become aware of your current strengths and weaknesses, the journal will ask you the following:

> What specific drills can I implement, test and work on to improve on the above?

This format will help create a system for you to make consistent progress in your game with the data you have collected.

And that's it. Once you practice the system, it is simple.

Brief Overview:
How to use your golf journal

1) The journal is split into the five categories of your game. **LONG GAME, IRON GAME, WEDGE GAME, GREENSIDE,** and **PUTTING.**

2) Under each category of your game are subtitles. In the LONG GAME and IRON GAME are subtitles **"LEFT"** and **"RIGHT."** In the WEDGE GAME, GREENSIDE and PUTTING are subtitled **"SHORT"** and **"LONG."**

   Dispersion left or right is important, but long and short are also two variables which are critical to your golfing success. Amateurs to professional golfers have greater dispersion left and right in the longer parts of their game, and bigger misses long and short in shorter parts of their game. The scale below them indicates how far you have hit your shot from your intended target. **Your intended target is where you want the ball to land and finish, not the flag/hole.**

3) In the middle of the page, you will find circles, above them are the specific distance from the shot which you hit from. So if you hit your tee shots in the region of (300-275 yards/meters) and hit your opening tee shot in your Club Championship 15 yards/meters left of your intended target, you would mark it with an (X) or a (dot) next to the number 15 on the left hand side of the scale. Shot by shot you will go through your round in the same way. From LONG GAME all the way through to PUTTING the ball in the hole. This is not to be done during your round as would only get in the way of the process. Sit down after your round with a cup of coffee or a glass of wine and enter your round. Being able to recall your shots is a great mental exercise as well.

4) By marking where your shots land relative to your intended target, with either a cross or a dot, will indicate what areas of your game are your strengths and your weaknesses at specific distances. The further your shots land towards the outside of the page, indicate areas of weakness. The closer your shots are to the center of the page, indicate the tighter the dispersion and proximity to your intended targets and highlight your strengths.

5) The number of fairways hit and greens in regulation per round are important facts, but they are also meaningless if you do not know any data behind it. Generating a report about your game this way, will enable you to work on specific areas of your game the next time you practice.

6) After every six rounds, your journal will ask you to complete the "80/20 Performance Review." Use this to highlight your strengths, weaknesses and any specific data to help plan your practice sessions and drills going forward.

7) On the right side of each page, you have an area to make notes on your performance for the given day. From things to work on to any emotions and feelings you felt out on the course that day.

   LET'S SEE WHAT A GOLF ENTRY LOOKS LIKE...

Welcome to The Masters

It is a very special day and you are teeing it up at Augusta Country Club.

The first hole is a Par 4, 445 yards long and you play it as follows:

Shot 1: 280 yards to 10 yards off intended target.
Shot 2: 165 yards to 12 yards right of the intended target and 8 yards short.
Shot 3: 12 yards to 2 yards to the hole.
Shot 4: In the hole.

This would be marked in your journal as the following:

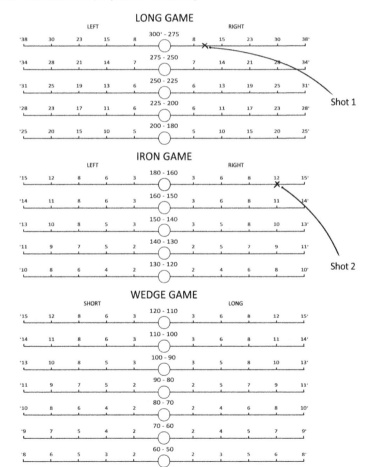

NOTES ON PERFORMANCE

- Kept routine and picked out specific targets despite feeling nervous.

- Didn't get greedy with the second shot, played it to the center of the green.

- Felt calm and relaxed out there.

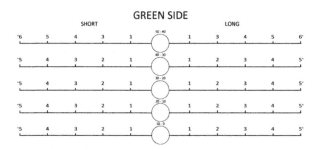

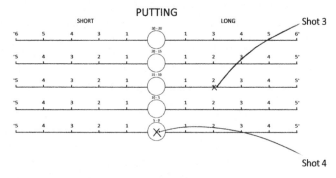

And that's it, you have successfully submitted one hole in your journal.

Trust me, once you get the hang of this it becomes really quick and easy :)

Let's see what a whole round looks like...

Course: Augusta   Score: 74   Date: 29 May

"Sometimes, things may not go your way, but the effort should be there every single night."

— MICHAEL JORDAN

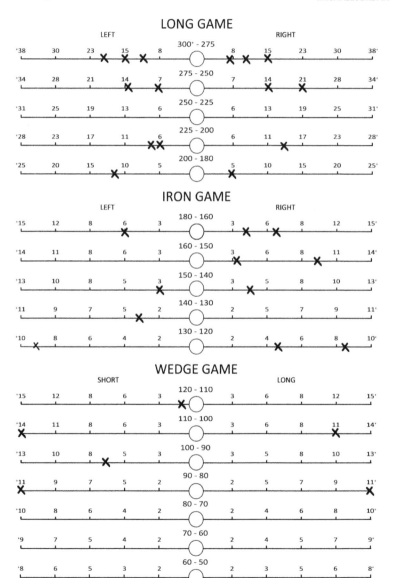

NOTES ON PERFORMANCE

- Drove the ball extremely well, felt very confident hitting a baby fade all day.

- Wedge game needs a lot of work, 100 yards and in was very poor.

- Speed felt way off on the greens, get to the course earlier next time and hit more puts.

- Felt calm focused out there, and at ease really enjoyed playing with Tom and Elsa. - Epic course!

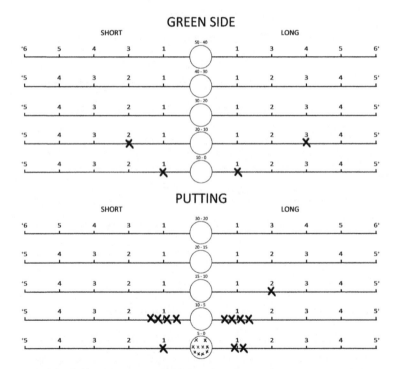

Now, based on the data collected above.
Lets see what a 80/20 Performance Review looks like...

How to get the most out of your 80/20 Performance Review

Dispersion Performance Review Example.

Best ways to discover and highlight your weaknesses can be to highlight or ring your shots that land towards the outer sides of the page. (See below)

Any shots that land in the last two numbers of either side of the page are worth highlighting as your weaknesses at any given yardage.

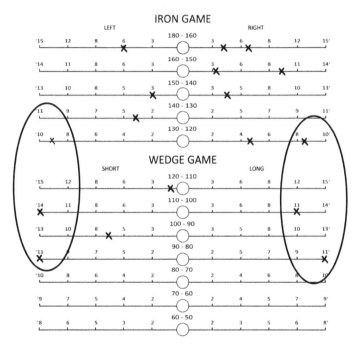

The next step is to transfer these yardages which you have ringed/ highlighted into the "Dispersion" section of the 80/20 Performance Review page, like below.

Which 20% of my yardages are resulting in 80% of my **DISPERSION** from the hole?

1) _130 - 120_

2) _110 - 100_

3) _90 - 80_

If all areas of your game are struggling, narrow your focus and keep asking yourself the question: **What 20% of my shots are resulting in 80% of my drop shots?**

You are looking for the leading domino, to ensure that every day you practice what matters most. When you know what matters most, everything makes sense. It is those who concentrate on but **one thing at a time** who advance in this world.

By highlighting the specific yardages which you have struggled at, you can appropriately plan how you are going to improve and turn these weaknesses of your game into a strength.

What specific drills can I implement, test and work on to improve on the above?

- *Still don't know my yardages well enough in wedge game, keep coming up long & short.*

- *Pace putting was way off, had no control with speed in which I was hitting my putts.*

WEDGE GAME:

1. Work on specific yardages and specific shots. Implement the clock face system, and know your yardages for 10, 11 and 12 o'clock swings.

2. Work on long distance lag puts before you compete to improve feel and speed on the greens.

You now have your next practice session planned, which is based on real data from your performance. No more guesswork, or tinkering on the range - 100% facts. When you have clear goals and know what to work on, you will come up with better answers to your problems.

The answer to getting better is getting to the heart of things by going small. Going small is ignoring all the things you could do, and getting to work on what you need to do.

It's recognizing that not all things matter equally in your game, and finding the things that matter most is your path to mastery. Extraordinary results are directly determined by how narrow you can make your focus.

You do exactly the same to highlight your strengths with the Proximity Performance Review page.

Dispersion
Performance Review

"Don't make friends who are comfortable to be with. Make friends who will force you to lever yourself up."
THOMAS J. WATSON

Which 20% of my yardages are resulting in 80% of my **DISPERSION** from the hole?

1) _130 - 120_
2) _110 - 100_
3) _90 - 80_
4) _10 - 5_
5) _5 - 0_

What specific drills can I implement, test and work on to improve on the above?

- Still don't know my yardages well enough in wedge game, keep coming up long & short.

- Pace putting was way off, had no control with speed I was hitting my putts.

WEDGE GAME:

1. Work on specific yardages and specific shots. Implement the clock face system, and know your yardages for 10, 11 and 12 o'clock swings.

2. Work on long distance lag putts before you compete to improve feel and speed on the greens.

Proximity
Performance Review

"Work gives you meaning and purpose and life is empty without it."
STEPHEN HAWKING

Which 20% of my yardages are resulting in 80% of my **PROXIMITY** from the hole?

1) 300 - 275
2) 275 - 250
3) 225 - 200
4) 200 - 180
5) 180 - 160

What specific drills can I implement, test and work on to improve on the above?

- Long game was really good, felt in full control off the tee and felt comfortable shaping the ball left and right

LONG GAME:

Don't change something that isn't working, keep doing the drills on the range - hitting it through specific target/ markers and recording your scores in your journal.

The majority of what you want will come from the minority of what you do. The key is to play the long game, and keep showing up over time. Success is built sequentially. It's one thing at a time. I hope this journal serves you and your game well.

To all your greatness on and off the fairways.

Kia kaha,
Chris Baker
MakingAClubChampion.com

For real round examples, tips and practical tips and drills to get the most out of your journal

visit:

www.makingaclubchampion.com/score-better-golf-journal

Course: _____ **Score:** _____ **Date:** _____

"There are no secrets to success. It is the result of preparation, hard work and learning from failure."

— COLIN POWELL

LONG GAME

LEFT					RIGHT			
				300' - 275				
'38	30	23	15	8 ○ 8	15	23	30	38'
				275 - 250				
'34	28	21	14	7 ○ 7	14	21	28	34'
				250 - 225				
'31	25	19	13	6 ○ 6	13	19	25	31'
				225 - 200				
'28	23	17	11	6 ○ 6	11	17	23	28'
				200 - 180				
'25	20	15	10	5 ○ 5	10	15	20	25'

IRON GAME

LEFT					RIGHT			
				180 - 160				
'15	12	8	6	3 ○ 3	6	8	12	15'
				160 - 150				
'14	11	8	6	3 ○ 3	6	8	11	14'
				150 - 140				
'13	10	8	5	3 ○ 3	5	8	10	13'
				140 - 130				
'11	9	7	5	2 ○ 2	5	7	9	11'
				130 - 120				
'10	8	6	4	2 ○ 2	4	6	8	10'

WEDGE GAME

SHORT					LONG			
				120 - 110				
'15	12	8	6	3 ○ 3	6	8	12	15'
				110 - 100				
'14	11	8	6	3 ○ 3	6	8	11	14'
				100 - 90				
'13	10	8	5	3 ○ 3	5	8	10	13'
				90 - 80				
'11	9	7	5	2 ○ 2	5	7	9	11'
				80 - 70				
'10	8	6	4	2 ○ 2	4	6	8	10'
				70 - 60				
'9	7	5	4	2 ○ 2	4	5	7	9'
				60 - 50				
'8	6	5	3	2 ○ 2	3	5	6	8'

NOTES ON PERFORMANCE

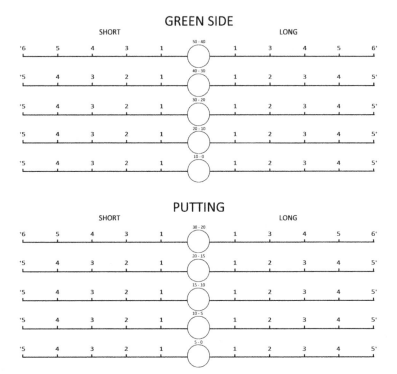

Course: _____ Score: _____ Date: _____

"Actions prove who someone is, words just prove who they want to be."

— UNKNOWN

LONG GAME

LEFT								RIGHT	

				300'-275					
'38	30	23	15	8	8	15	23	30	38'
'34	28	21	14	7 — 275-250 — 7		14	21	28	34'
'31	25	19	13	6 — 250-225 — 6		13	19	25	31'
'28	23	17	11	6 — 225-200 — 6		11	17	23	28'
'25	20	15	10	5 — 200-180 — 5		10	15	20	25'

IRON GAME

LEFT								RIGHT	
'15	12	8	6	3 — 180-160 — 3		6	8	12	15'
'14	11	8	6	3 — 160-150 — 3		6	8	11	14'
'13	10	8	5	3 — 150-140 — 3		5	8	10	13'
'11	9	7	5	2 — 140-130 — 2		5	7	9	11'
'10	8	6	4	2 — 130-120 — 2		4	6	8	10'

WEDGE GAME

SHORT								LONG	
'15	12	8	6	3 — 120-110 — 3		6	8	12	15'
'14	11	8	6	3 — 110-100 — 3		6	8	11	14'
'13	10	8	5	3 — 100-90 — 3		5	8	10	13'
'11	9	7	5	2 — 90-80 — 2		5	7	9	11'
'10	8	6	4	2 — 80-70 — 2		4	6	8	10'
'9	7	5	4	2 — 70-60 — 2		4	5	7	9'
'8	6	5	3	2 — 60-50 — 2		3	5	6	8'

NOTES ON PERFORMANCE

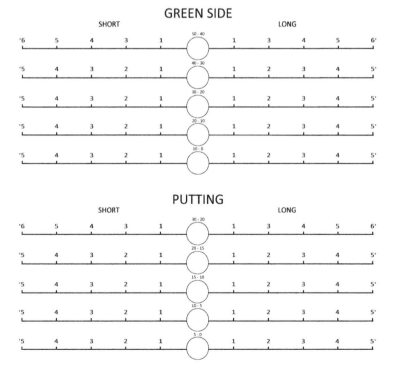

Course: _____ **Score:** _____ **Date:** _____

"Sometimes, things may not go your way, but the effort should be there every single night."

— MICHAEL JORDAN

LONG GAME

LEFT						RIGHT			
'38	30	23	15	8	300' - 275 ○ 8	15	23	30	38'
'34	28	21	14	7	275 - 250 ○ 7	14	21	28	34'
'31	25	19	13	6	250 - 225 ○ 6	13	19	25	31'
'28	23	17	11	6	225 - 200 ○ 6	11	17	23	28'
'25	20	15	10	5	200 - 180 ○ 5	10	15	20	25'

IRON GAME

LEFT						RIGHT			
'15	12	8	6	3	180 - 160 ○ 3	6	8	12	15'
'14	11	8	6	3	160 - 150 ○ 3	6	8	11	14'
'13	10	8	5	3	150 - 140 ○ 3	5	8	10	13'
'11	9	7	5	2	140 - 130 ○ 2	5	7	9	11'
'10	8	6	4	2	130 - 120 ○ 2	4	6	8	10'

WEDGE GAME

SHORT						LONG			
'15	12	8	6	3	120 - 110 ○ 3	6	8	12	15'
'14	11	8	6	3	110 - 100 ○ 3	6	8	11	14'
'13	10	8	5	3	100 - 90 ○ 3	5	8	10	13'
'11	9	7	5	2	90 - 80 ○ 2	5	7	9	11'
'10	8	6	4	2	80 - 70 ○ 2	4	6	8	10'
'9	7	5	4	2	70 - 60 ○ 2	4	5	7	9'
'8	6	5	3	2	60 - 50 ○ 2	3	5	6	8'

NOTES ON PERFORMANCE

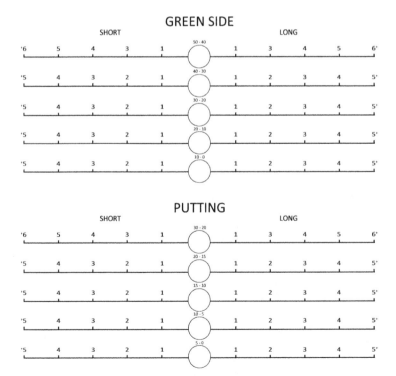

Course: _____ Score: _____ Date: _____

"There is only one thing that makes a dream impossible to achieve: the fear of failure."

- PAULO COELHO

LONG GAME

LEFT					RIGHT			
				300' - 275				
'38	30	23	15	8 ○ 8	15	23	30	38'
				275 - 250				
'34	28	21	14	7 ○ 7	14	21	28	34'
				250 - 225				
'31	25	19	13	6 ○ 6	13	19	25	31'
				225 - 200				
'28	23	17	11	6 ○ 6	11	17	23	28'
				200 - 180				
'25	20	15	10	5 ○ 5	10	15	20	25'

IRON GAME

LEFT					RIGHT			
				180 - 160				
'15	12	8	6	3 ○ 3	6	8	12	15'
				160 - 150				
'14	11	8	6	3 ○ 3	6	8	11	14'
				150 - 140				
'13	10	8	5	3 ○ 3	5	8	10	13'
				140 - 130				
'11	9	7	5	2 ○ 2	5	7	9	11'
				130 - 120				
'10	8	6	4	2 ○ 2	4	6	8	10'

WEDGE GAME

SHORT					LONG			
				120 - 110				
'15	12	8	6	3 ○ 3	6	8	12	15'
				110 - 100				
'14	11	8	6	3 ○ 3	6	8	11	14'
				100 - 90				
'13	10	8	5	3 ○ 3	5	8	10	13'
				90 - 80				
'11	9	7	5	2 ○ 2	5	7	9	11'
				80 - 70				
'10	8	6	4	2 ○ 2	4	6	8	10'
				70 - 60				
'9	7	5	4	2 ○ 2	4	5	7	9'
				60 - 50				
'8	6	5	3	2 ○ 2	3	5	6	8'

NOTES ON PERFORMANCE

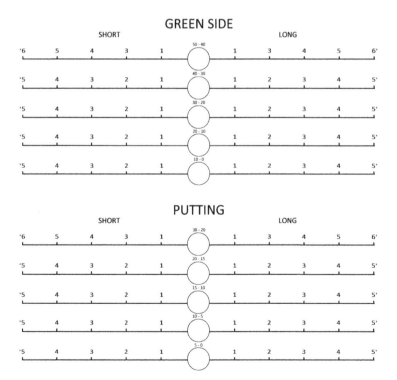

Course: _____ Score: _____ Date: _____

"Productivity is being able to do things that you were never able to do before."

- FRANZ KAFKA

LONG GAME

LEFT								RIGHT	
				300' - 275					
'38	30	23	15	8	8	15	23	30	38'
				275 - 250					
'34	28	21	14	7	7	14	21	28	34'
				250 - 225					
'31	25	19	13	6	6	13	19	25	31'
				225 - 200					
'28	23	17	11	6	6	11	17	23	28'
				200 - 180					
'25	20	15	10	5	5	10	15	20	25'

IRON GAME

LEFT								RIGHT	
				180 - 160					
'15	12	8	6	3	3	6	8	12	15'
				160 - 150					
'14	11	8	6	3	3	6	8	11	14'
				150 - 140					
'13	10	8	5	3	3	5	8	10	13'
				140 - 130					
'11	9	7	5	2	2	5	7	9	11'
				130 - 120					
'10	8	6	4	2	2	4	6	8	10'

WEDGE GAME

SHORT								LONG	
				120 - 110					
'15	12	8	6	3	3	6	8	12	15'
				110 - 100					
'14	11	8	6	3	3	6	8	11	14'
				100 - 90					
'13	10	8	5	3	3	5	8	10	13'
				90 - 80					
'11	9	7	5	2	2	5	7	9	11'
				80 - 70					
'10	8	6	4	2	2	4	6	8	10'
				70 - 60					
'9	7	5	4	2	2	4	5	7	9'
				60 - 50					
'8	6	5	3	2	2	3	5	6	8'

NOTES ON PERFORMANCE

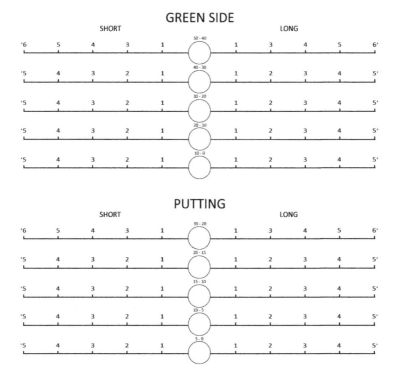

Course: _____   Score: _____   Date: _____

"Don't worry what others are doing. Do you!"

- RUSSELL SIMMONS

LONG GAME

		LEFT			300+ - 275			RIGHT		
'38	30	23	15	8	○	8	15	23	30	38'
'34	28	21	14	7	275 - 250 ○	7	14	21	28	34'
'31	25	19	13	6	250 - 225 ○	6	13	19	25	31'
'28	23	17	11	6	225 - 200 ○	6	11	17	23	28'
'25	20	15	10	5	200 - 180 ○	5	10	15	20	25'

IRON GAME

		LEFT						RIGHT		
'15	12	8	6	3	180 - 160 ○	3	6	8	12	15'
'14	11	8	6	3	160 - 150 ○	3	6	8	11	14'
'13	10	8	5	3	150 - 140 ○	3	5	8	10	13'
'11	9	7	5	2	140 - 130 ○	2	5	7	9	11'
'10	8	6	4	2	130 - 120 ○	2	4	6	8	10'

WEDGE GAME

		SHORT						LONG		
'15	12	8	6	3	120 - 110 ○	3	6	8	12	15'
'14	11	8	6	3	110 - 100 ○	3	6	8	11	14'
'13	10	8	5	3	100 - 90 ○	3	5	8	10	13'
'11	9	7	5	2	90 - 80 ○	2	5	7	9	11'
'10	8	6	4	2	80 - 70 ○	2	4	6	8	10'
'9	7	5	4	2	70 - 60 ○	2	4	5	7	9'
'8	6	5	3	2	60 - 50 ○	2	3	5	6	8'

NOTES ON PERFORMANCE

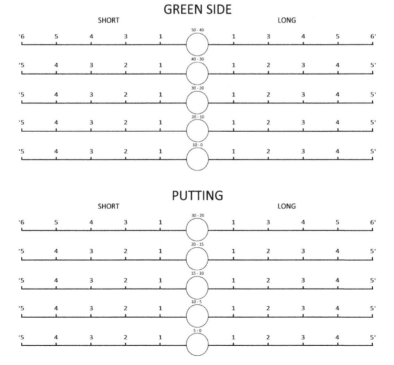

DISPERSION PERFORMANCE REVIEW

"We create success or failure on the course primarily by our thoughts."
GARY PLAYER

Which 20% of my yardages are resulting in 80% of my DISPERSION from the hole?

1) _____

2) _____

3) _____

4) _____

5) _____

What specific drills can I implement, test and work on to improve on the above?

_____

_____

_____

_____

PROXIMITY PERFORMANCE REVIEW

"Always make a total effort, even when the odds are against you."
ARNOLD PALMER

Which 20% of my yardages are resulting in 80% of my **PROXIMITY** from the hole?

1) _____

2) _____

3) _____

4) _____

5) _____

What specific drills can I implement, test and work on to improve on the above?

_____

_____

_____

_____

Course: _____ Score: _____ Date: _____

"Just remember The people that say, 'your dreams are impossible' have already quit on theirs."

- GRANT CARDONE

LONG GAME

LEFT								RIGHT	
'38	30	23	15	8	300' - 275	8	15	23	30	38'
'34	28	21	14	7	275 - 250	7	14	21	28	34'
'31	25	19	13	6	250 - 225	6	13	19	25	31'
'28	23	17	11	6	225 - 200	6	11	17	23	28'
'25	20	15	10	5	200 - 180	5	10	15	20	25'

IRON GAME

LEFT								RIGHT	
'15	12	8	6	3	180 - 160	3	6	8	12	15'
'14	11	8	6	3	160 - 150	3	6	8	11	14'
'13	10	8	5	3	150 - 140	3	5	8	10	13'
'11	9	7	5	2	140 - 130	2	5	7	9	11'
'10	8	6	4	2	130 - 120	2	4	6	8	10'

WEDGE GAME

SHORT								LONG	
'15	12	8	6	3	120 - 110	3	6	8	12	15'
'14	11	8	6	3	110 - 100	3	6	8	11	14'
'13	10	8	5	3	100 - 90	3	5	8	10	13'
'11	9	7	5	2	90 - 80	2	5	7	9	11'
'10	8	6	4	2	80 - 70	2	4	6	8	10'
'9	7	5	4	2	70 - 60	2	4	5	7	9'
'8	6	5	3	2	60 - 50	2	3	5	6	8'

NOTES ON PERFORMANCE

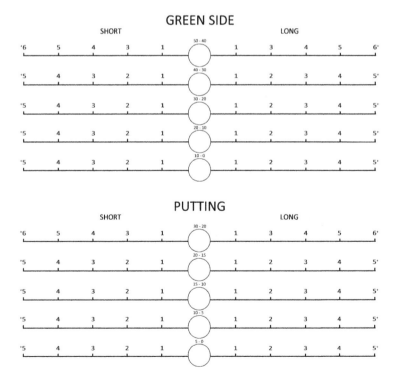

Course: Score: Date:

"Show me a guy who's afraid to look bad, and I'll show you a guy you can beat every time."

- LOU BROCK

LONG GAME

		LEFT					RIGHT		
'38	30	23	15	8	**300⁺ - 275** ◯ 8	15	23	30	38'
'34	28	21	14	7	**275 - 250** ◯ 7	14	21	28	34'
'31	25	19	13	6	**250 - 225** ◯ 6	13	19	25	31'
'28	23	17	11	6	**225 - 200** ◯ 6	11	17	23	28'
'25	20	15	10	5	**200 - 180** ◯ 5	10	15	20	25'

IRON GAME

		LEFT					RIGHT		
'15	12	8	6	3	**180 - 160** ◯ 3	6	8	12	15'
'14	11	8	6	3	**160 - 150** ◯ 3	6	8	11	14'
'13	10	8	5	3	**150 - 140** ◯ 3	5	8	10	13'
'11	9	7	5	2	**140 - 130** ◯ 2	5	7	9	11'
'10	8	6	4	2	**130 - 120** ◯ 2	4	6	8	10'

WEDGE GAME

		SHORT					LONG		
'15	12	8	6	3	**120 - 110** ◯ 3	6	8	12	15'
'14	11	8	6	3	**110 - 100** ◯ 3	6	8	11	14'
'13	10	8	5	3	**100 - 90** ◯ 3	5	8	10	13'
'11	9	7	5	2	**90 - 80** ◯ 2	5	7	9	11'
'10	8	6	4	2	**80 - 70** ◯ 2	4	6	8	10'
'9	7	5	4	2	**70 - 60** ◯ 2	4	5	7	9'
'8	6	5	3	2	**60 - 50** ◯ 2	3	5	6	8'

NOTES ON PERFORMANCE

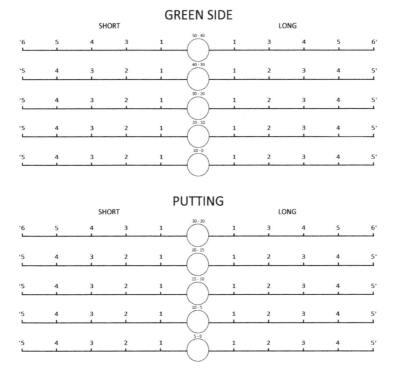

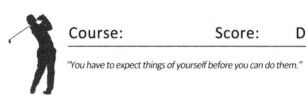

Course: _____ **Score:** _____ **Date:** _____

"You have to expect things of yourself before you can do them."

- MICHAEL JORDAN

LONG GAME

LEFT						RIGHT			
					300' - 275				
'38	30	23	15	8	○	8	15	23	30	38'
					275 - 250				
'34	28	21	14	7	○	7	14	21	28	34'
					250 - 225				
'31	25	19	13	6	○	6	13	19	25	31'
					225 - 200				
'28	23	17	11	6	○	6	11	17	23	28'
					200 - 180				
'25	20	15	10	5	○	5	10	15	20	25'

IRON GAME

LEFT						RIGHT			
					180 - 160				
'15	12	8	6	3	○	3	6	8	12	15'
					160 - 150				
'14	11	8	6	3	○	3	6	8	11	14'
					150 - 140				
'13	10	8	5	3	○	3	5	8	10	13'
					140 - 130				
'11	9	7	5	2	○	2	5	7	9	11'
					130 - 120				
'10	8	6	4	2	○	2	4	6	8	10'

WEDGE GAME

SHORT						LONG			
					120 - 110				
'15	12	8	6	3	○	3	6	8	12	15'
					110 - 100				
'14	11	8	6	3	○	3	6	8	11	14'
					100 - 90				
'13	10	8	5	3	○	3	5	8	10	13'
					90 - 80				
'11	9	7	5	2	○	2	5	7	9	11'
					80 - 70				
'10	8	6	4	2	○	2	4	6	8	10'
					70 - 60				
'9	7	5	4	2	○	2	4	5	7	9'
					60 - 50				
'8	6	5	3	2	○	2	3	5	6	8'

NOTES ON PERFORMANCE

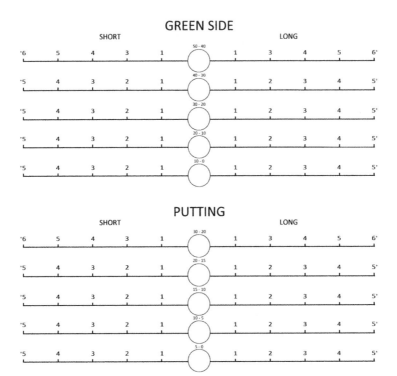

Course: _____   Score: _____   Date: _____

"Imagine Your Life Is Perfect In Every Respect; What Would It Look Like?"

— BRIAN TRACY

LONG GAME

LEFT						RIGHT			
'38	30	23	15	8	300' - 275	8	15	23	30	38'
'34	28	21	14	7	275 - 250	7	14	21	28	34'
'31	25	19	13	6	250 - 225	6	13	19	25	31'
'28	23	17	11	6	225 - 200	6	11	17	23	28'
'25	20	15	10	5	200 - 180	5	10	15	20	25'

IRON GAME

LEFT						RIGHT			
'15	12	8	6	3	180 - 160	3	6	8	12	15'
'14	11	8	6	3	160 - 150	3	6	8	11	14'
'13	10	8	5	3	150 - 140	3	5	8	10	13'
'11	9	7	5	2	140 - 130	2	5	7	9	11'
'10	8	6	4	2	130 - 120	2	4	6	8	10'

WEDGE GAME

SHORT						LONG			
'15	12	8	6	3	120 - 110	3	6	8	12	15'
'14	11	8	6	3	110 - 100	3	6	8	11	14'
'13	10	8	5	3	100 - 90	3	5	8	10	13'
'11	9	7	5	2	90 - 80	2	5	7	9	11'
'10	8	6	4	2	80 - 70	2	4	6	8	10'
'9	7	5	4	2	70 - 60	2	4	5	7	9'
'8	6	5	3	2	60 - 50	2	3	5	6	8'

NOTES ON PERFORMANCE

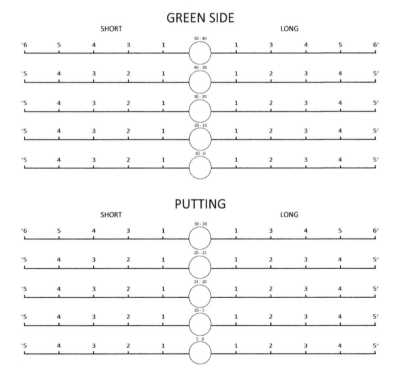

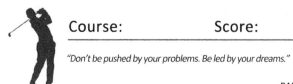

Course: _____   Score: _____   Date: _____

"Don't be pushed by your problems. Be led by your dreams."

- RALPH WALDO EMERSON

LONG GAME

	LEFT							RIGHT		
'38	30	23	15	8	300⁺ - 275	8	15	23	30	38'
'34	28	21	14	7	275 - 250	7	14	21	28	34'
'31	25	19	13	6	250 - 225	6	13	19	25	31'
'28	23	17	11	6	225 - 200	6	11	17	23	28'
'25	20	15	10	5	200 - 180	5	10	15	20	25'

IRON GAME

	LEFT							RIGHT		
'15	12	8	6	3	180 - 160	3	6	8	12	15'
'14	11	8	6	3	160 - 150	3	6	8	11	14'
'13	10	8	5	3	150 - 140	3	5	8	10	13'
'11	9	7	5	2	140 - 130	2	5	7	9	11'
'10	8	6	4	2	130 - 120	2	4	6	8	10'

WEDGE GAME

	SHORT							LONG		
'15	12	8	6	3	120 - 110	3	6	8	12	15'
'14	11	8	6	3	110 - 100	3	6	8	11	14'
'13	10	8	5	3	100 - 90	3	5	8	10	13'
'11	9	7	5	2	90 - 80	2	5	7	9	11'
'10	8	6	4	2	80 - 70	2	4	6	8	10'
'9	7	5	4	2	70 - 60	2	4	5	7	9'
'8	6	5	3	2	60 - 50	2	3	5	6	8'

NOTES ON PERFORMANCE

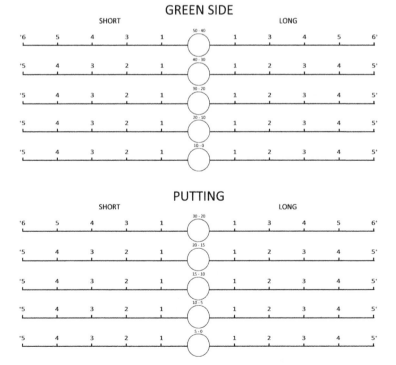

Course: _____ Score: _____ Date: _____

"Excellence is the gradual result of always striving to do better."

— PAT RILEY

LONG GAME

LEFT					RIGHT			
				300'-275				
'38	30	23	15	8 ◯ 8	15	23	30	38'
				275-250				
'34	28	21	14	7 ◯ 7	14	21	28	34'
				250-225				
'31	25	19	13	6 ◯ 6	13	19	25	31'
				225-200				
'28	23	17	11	6 ◯ 6	11	17	23	28'
				200-180				
'25	20	15	10	5 ◯ 5	10	15	20	25'

IRON GAME

LEFT					RIGHT			
				180-160				
'15	12	8	6	3 ◯ 3	6	8	12	15'
				160-150				
'14	11	8	6	3 ◯ 3	6	8	11	14'
				150-140				
'13	10	8	5	3 ◯ 3	5	8	10	13'
				140-130				
'11	9	7	5	2 ◯ 2	5	7	9	11'
				130-120				
'10	8	6	4	2 ◯ 2	4	6	8	10'

WEDGE GAME

SHORT					LONG			
				120-110				
'15	12	8	6	3 ◯ 3	6	8	12	15'
				110-100				
'14	11	8	6	3 ◯ 3	6	8	11	14'
				100-90				
'13	10	8	5	3 ◯ 3	5	8	10	13'
				90-80				
'11	9	7	5	2 ◯ 2	5	7	9	11'
				80-70				
'10	8	6	4	2 ◯ 2	4	6	8	10'
				70-60				
'9	7	5	4	2 ◯ 2	4	5	7	9'
				60-50				
'8	6	5	3	2 ◯ 2	3	5	6	8'

NOTES ON PERFORMANCE

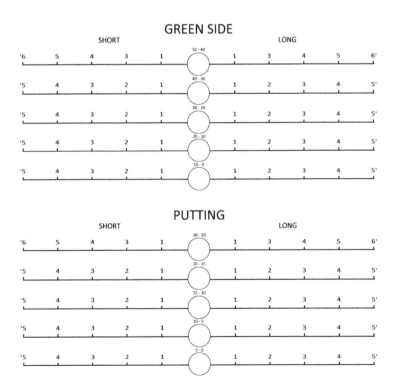

DISPERSION PERFORMANCE REVIEW

"If you really want to do something you'll find a way, if you don't you'll find an excuse."
JIM ROHN

Which 20% of my yardages are resulting in 80% of my DISPERSION from the hole?

1) _____

2) _____

3) _____

4) _____

5) _____

What specific drills can I implement, test and work on to improve on the above?

_____

_____

_____

_____

PROXIMITY PERFORMANCE REVIEW

"People Who Are Crazy Enough To Think They Can Change The World, Are The Ones Who Do."
ROB SILTANEN

Which 20% of my yardages are resulting in 80% of my **PROXIMITY** from the hole?

1) _____
2) _____
3) _____
4) _____
5) _____

What specific drills can I implement, test and work on to improve on the above?

_____
_____
_____
_____

Course: _____ **Score:** _____ **Date:** _____

"Success consists of going from failure to failure without loss of enthusiasm."

— WINSTON CHURCHILL

LONG GAME

LEFT					RIGHT			
'38	30	23	15	8 — 300'-275 — 8	15	23	30	38'
'34	28	21	14	7 — 275-250 — 7	14	21	28	34'
'31	25	19	13	6 — 250-225 — 6	13	19	25	31'
'28	23	17	11	6 — 225-200 — 6	11	17	23	28'
'25	20	15	10	5 — 200-180 — 5	10	15	20	25'

IRON GAME

LEFT					RIGHT			
'15	12	8	6	3 — 180-160 — 3	6	8	12	15'
'14	11	8	6	3 — 160-150 — 3	6	8	11	14'
'13	10	8	5	3 — 150-140 — 3	5	8	10	13'
'11	9	7	5	2 — 140-130 — 2	5	7	9	11'
'10	8	6	4	2 — 130-120 — 2	4	6	8	10'

WEDGE GAME

SHORT					LONG			
'15	12	8	6	3 — 120-110 — 3	6	8	12	15'
'14	11	8	6	3 — 110-100 — 3	6	8	11	14'
'13	10	8	5	3 — 100-90 — 3	5	8	10	13'
'11	9	7	5	2 — 90-80 — 2	5	7	9	11'
'10	8	6	4	2 — 80-70 — 2	4	6	8	10'
'9	7	5	4	2 — 70-60 — 2	4	5	7	9'
'8	6	5	3	2 — 60-50 — 2	3	5	6	8'

NOTES ON PERFORMANCE

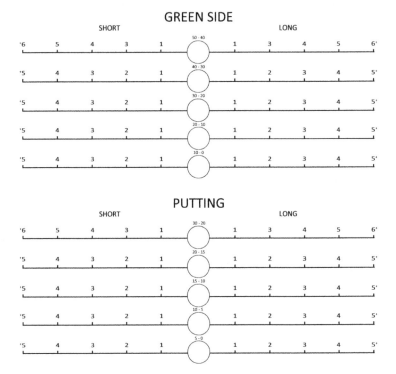

Course: _____ Score: _____ Date: _____

"Whether You Think You Can Or Think You Can't, You're Right."

- HENRY FORD

LONG GAME

LEFT				300' - 275			RIGHT	
'38	30	23	15	8 ○ 8	15	23	30	38'
'34	28	21	14	7 275 - 250 7	14	21	28	34'
				○				
'31	25	19	13	6 250 - 225 6	13	19	25	31'
				○				
'28	23	17	11	6 225 - 200 6	11	17	23	28'
				○				
'25	20	15	10	5 200 - 180 5	10	15	20	25'
				○				

IRON GAME

LEFT				180 - 160			RIGHT	
'15	12	8	6	3 ○ 3	6	8	12	15'
'14	11	8	6	3 160 - 150 3	6	8	11	14'
				○				
'13	10	8	5	3 150 - 140 3	5	8	10	13'
				○				
'11	9	7	5	2 140 - 130 2	5	7	9	11'
				○				
'10	8	6	4	2 130 - 120 2	4	6	8	10'
				○				

WEDGE GAME

SHORT				120 - 110			LONG	
'15	12	8	6	3 ○ 3	6	8	12	15'
'14	11	8	6	3 110 - 100 3	6	8	11	14'
				○				
'13	10	8	5	3 100 - 90 3	5	8	10	13'
				○				
'11	9	7	5	2 90 - 80 2	5	7	9	11'
				○				
'10	8	6	4	2 80 - 70 2	4	6	8	10'
				○				
'9	7	5	4	2 70 - 60 2	4	5	7	9'
				○				
'8	6	5	3	2 60 - 50 2	3	5	6	8'
				○				

NOTES ON PERFORMANCE

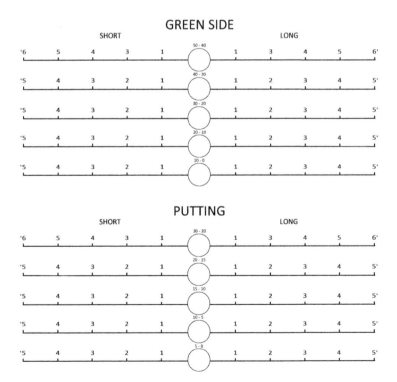

Course: _____ Score: _____ Date: _____

"You Are Never Too Old To Set Another Goal Or To Dream A New Dream."

- C.S. LEWIS

LONG GAME

LEFT					300' - 275			RIGHT		
'38	30	23	15	8	◯	8	15	23	30	38'
'34	28	21	14	7	275 - 250 ◯	7	14	21	28	34'
'31	25	19	13	6	250 - 225 ◯	6	13	19	25	31'
'28	23	17	11	6	225 - 200 ◯	6	11	17	23	28'
'25	20	15	10	5	200 - 180 ◯	5	10	15	20	25'

IRON GAME

LEFT					180 - 160			RIGHT		
'15	12	8	6	3	◯	3	6	8	12	15'
'14	11	8	6	3	160 - 150 ◯	3	6	8	11	14'
'13	10	8	5	3	150 - 140 ◯	3	5	8	10	13'
'11	9	7	5	2	140 - 130 ◯	2	5	7	9	11'
'10	8	6	4	2	130 - 120 ◯	2	4	6	8	10'

WEDGE GAME

SHORT					120 - 110			LONG		
'15	12	8	6	3	◯	3	6	8	12	15'
'14	11	8	6	3	110 - 100 ◯	3	6	8	11	14'
'13	10	8	5	3	100 - 90 ◯	3	5	8	10	13'
'11	9	7	5	2	90 - 80 ◯	2	5	7	9	11'
'10	8	6	4	2	80 - 70 ◯	2	4	6	8	10'
'9	7	5	4	2	70 - 60 ◯	2	4	5	7	9'
'8	6	5	3	2	60 - 50 ◯	2	3	5	6	8'

NOTES ON PERFORMANCE

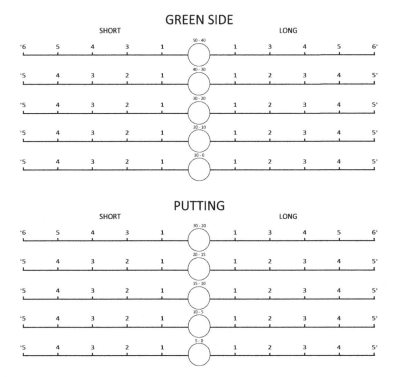

Course: _____ Score: _____ Date: _____

"I Think Goals Should Never Be Easy, They Should Force You To Work, Even If They Are Uncomfortable At The Time."

- MICHAEL PHELPS

LONG GAME

LEFT					300+ - 275				RIGHT	
'38	30	23	15	8	○	8	15	23	30	38'
'34	28	21	14	7	275 - 250 ○	7	14	21	28	34'
'31	25	19	13	6	250 - 225 ○	6	13	19	25	31'
'28	23	17	11	6	225 - 200 ○	6	11	17	23	28'
'25	20	15	10	5	200 - 180 ○	5	10	15	20	25'

IRON GAME

LEFT					180 - 160				RIGHT	
'15	12	8	6	3	○	3	6	8	12	15'
'14	11	8	6	3	160 - 150 ○	3	6	8	11	14'
'13	10	8	5	3	150 - 140 ○	3	5	8	10	13'
'11	9	7	5	2	140 - 130 ○	2	5	7	9	11'
'10	8	6	4	2	130 - 120 ○	2	4	6	8	10'

WEDGE GAME

SHORT					120 - 110				LONG	
'15	12	8	6	3	○	3	6	8	12	15'
'14	11	8	6	3	110 - 100 ○	3	6	8	11	14'
'13	10	8	5	3	100 - 90 ○	3	5	8	10	13'
'11	9	7	5	2	90 - 80 ○	2	5	7	9	11'
'10	8	6	4	2	80 - 70 ○	2	4	6	8	10'
'9	7	5	4	2	70 - 60 ○	2	4	5	7	9'
'8	6	5	3	2	60 - 50 ○	2	3	5	6	8'

NOTES ON PERFORMANCE

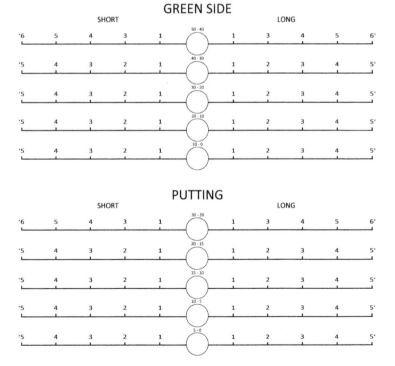

Course: _____ Score: _____ Date: _____

"In the middle of every difficulty lies opportunity."

— ALBERT EINSTEIN

LONG GAME

LEFT						RIGHT			
					300+ – 275				
'38	30	23	15	8	○	8	15	23	30	38'
					275 – 250				
'34	28	21	14	7	○	7	14	21	28	34'
					250 – 225				
'31	25	19	13	6	○	6	13	19	25	31'
					225 – 200				
'28	23	17	11	6	○	6	11	17	23	28'
					200 – 180				
'25	20	15	10	5	○	5	10	15	20	25'

IRON GAME

LEFT						RIGHT			
					180 – 160				
'15	12	8	6	3	○	3	6	8	12	15'
					160 – 150				
'14	11	8	6	3	○	3	6	8	11	14'
					150 – 140				
'13	10	8	5	3	○	3	5	8	10	13'
					140 – 130				
'11	9	7	5	2	○	2	5	7	9	11'
					130 – 120				
'10	8	6	4	2	○	2	4	6	8	10'

WEDGE GAME

SHORT						LONG			
					120 – 110				
'15	12	8	6	3	○	3	6	8	12	15'
					110 – 100				
'14	11	8	6	3	○	3	6	8	11	14'
					100 – 90				
'13	10	8	5	3	○	3	5	8	10	13'
					90 – 80				
'11	9	7	5	2	○	2	5	7	9	11'
					80 – 70				
'10	8	6	4	2	○	2	4	6	8	10'
					70 – 60				
'9	7	5	4	2	○	2	4	5	7	9'
					60 – 50				
'8	6	5	3	2	○	2	3	5	6	8'

NOTES ON PERFORMANCE

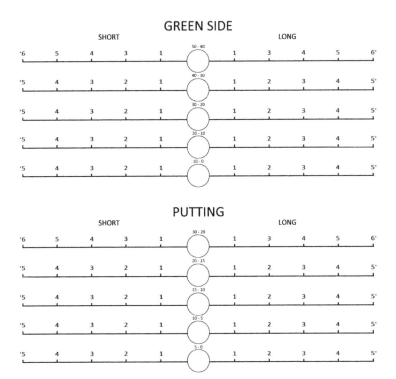

Course: **Score:** **Date:**

"Never ignore someone who cares for you because someday you'll realize you've lost a diamond while you were busy collecting stones."

— UNKNOWN

LONG GAME

	LEFT						RIGHT		
					300' – 275				
'38	30	23	15	8	○	8	15	23	30	38'
					275 – 250				
'34	28	21	14	7	○	7	14	21	28	34'
					250 – 225				
'31	25	19	13	6	○	6	13	19	25	31'
					225 – 200				
'28	23	17	11	6	○	6	11	17	23	28'
					200 – 180				
'25	20	15	10	5	○	5	10	15	20	25'

IRON GAME

	LEFT						RIGHT		
					180 – 160				
'15	12	8	6	3	○	3	6	8	12	15'
					160 – 150				
'14	11	8	6	3	○	3	6	8	11	14'
					150 – 140				
'13	10	8	5	3	○	3	5	8	10	13'
					140 – 130				
'11	9	7	5	2	○	2	5	7	9	11'
					130 – 120				
'10	8	6	4	2	○	2	4	6	8	10'

WEDGE GAME

	SHORT						LONG		
					120 – 110				
'15	12	8	6	3	○	3	6	8	12	15'
					110 – 100				
'14	11	8	6	3	○	3	6	8	11	14'
					100 – 90				
'13	10	8	5	3	○	3	5	8	10	13'
					90 – 80				
'11	9	7	5	2	○	2	5	7	9	11'
					80 – 70				
'10	8	6	4	2	○	2	4	6	8	10'
					70 – 60				
'9	7	5	4	2	○	2	4	5	7	9'
					60 – 50				
'8	6	5	3	2	○	2	3	5	6	8'

NOTES ON PERFORMANCE

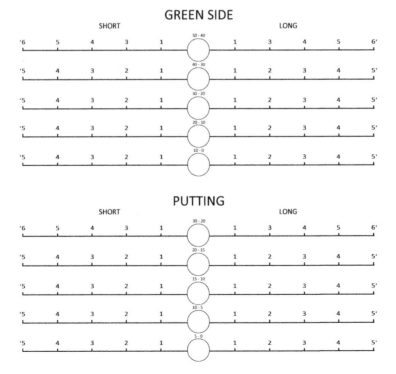

DISPERSION PERFORMANCE REVIEW

"In every day, there are 1,440 minutes. That means we have 1,440 daily opportunities to make a positive impact."
LES BROWN

Which 20% of my yardages are resulting in 80% of my DISPERSION from the hole?

1) _____

2) _____

3) _____

4) _____

5) _____

What specific drills can I implement, test and work on to improve on the above?

_____

_____

_____

_____

PROXIMITY PERFORMANCE REVIEW

"If we don't change, we don't grow. If we don't grow, we aren't really living."
GAIL SHEEHY

Which 20% of my yardages are resulting in 80% of my **PROXIMITY** from the hole?

1) _____
2) _____
3) _____
4) _____
5) _____

What specific drills can I implement, test and work on to improve on the above?

_____
_____
_____
_____

Course: _____ Score: _____ Date: _____

"Do not go where the path may lead, go instead where there is no path and leave a trail."

— RALPH WALDO EMERSON

LONG GAME

LEFT						RIGHT			
					300' - 275				
'38	30	23	15	8	○	8	15	23	30	38'
					275 - 250				
'34	28	21	14	7	○	7	14	21	28	34'
					250 - 225				
'31	25	19	13	6	○	6	13	19	25	31'
					225 - 200				
'28	23	17	11	6	○	6	11	17	23	28'
					200 - 180				
'25	20	15	10	5	○	5	10	15	20	25'

IRON GAME

LEFT						RIGHT			
					180 - 160				
'15	12	8	6	3	○	3	6	8	12	15'
					160 - 150				
'14	11	8	6	3	○	3	6	8	11	14'
					150 - 140				
'13	10	8	5	3	○	3	5	8	10	13'
					140 - 130				
'11	9	7	5	2	○	2	5	7	9	11'
					130 - 120				
'10	8	6	4	2	○	2	4	6	8	10'

WEDGE GAME

SHORT						LONG			
					120 - 110				
'15	12	8	6	3	○	3	6	8	12	15'
					110 - 100				
'14	11	8	6	3	○	3	6	8	11	14'
					100 - 90				
'13	10	8	5	3	○	3	5	8	10	13'
					90 - 80				
'11	9	7	5	2	○	2	5	7	9	11'
					80 - 70				
'10	8	6	4	2	○	2	4	6	8	10'
					70 - 60				
'9	7	5	4	2	○	2	4	5	7	9'
					60 - 50				
'8	6	5	3	2	○	2	3	5	6	8'

NOTES ON PERFORMANCE

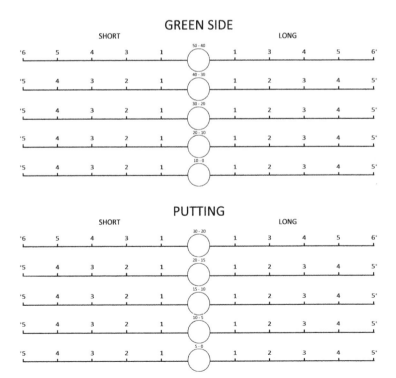

Course: _____ Score: _____ Date: _____

"You Don't Have To Be Great To Start, But You Have To Start To Be Great."

- ZIG ZIGLAR

LONG GAME

LEFT						RIGHT			
'38	30	23	15	8	**300' - 275**	8	15	23	30	38'
'34	28	21	14	7	**275 - 250**	7	14	21	28	34'
'31	25	19	13	6	**250 - 225**	6	13	19	25	31'
'28	23	17	11	6	**225 - 200**	6	11	17	23	28'
'25	20	15	10	5	**200 - 180**	5	10	15	20	25'

IRON GAME

LEFT						RIGHT			
'15	12	8	6	3	**180 - 160**	3	6	8	12	15'
'14	11	8	6	3	**160 - 150**	3	6	8	11	14'
'13	10	8	5	3	**150 - 140**	3	5	8	10	13'
'11	9	7	5	2	**140 - 130**	2	5	7	9	11'
'10	8	6	4	2	**130 - 120**	2	4	6	8	10'

WEDGE GAME

SHORT						LONG			
'15	12	8	6	3	**120 - 110**	3	6	8	12	15'
'14	11	8	6	3	**110 - 100**	3	6	8	11	14'
'13	10	8	5	3	**100 - 90**	3	5	8	10	13'
'11	9	7	5	2	**90 - 80**	2	5	7	9	11'
'10	8	6	4	2	**80 - 70**	2	4	6	8	10'
'9	7	5	4	2	**70 - 60**	2	4	5	7	9'
'8	6	5	3	2	**60 - 50**	2	3	5	6	8'

NOTES ON PERFORMANCE

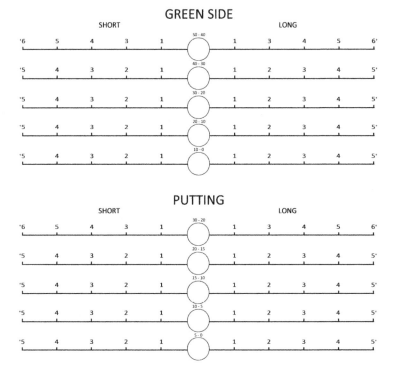

Course: _____ Score: _____ Date: _____

"Keep your eyes on the stars and your feet on the ground."

\- THEODORE ROOSEVELT

LONG GAME

		LEFT						RIGHT		
					300'+ - 275					
'38	30	23	15	8	○	8	15	23	30	38'
					275 - 250					
'34	28	21	14	7	○	7	14	21	28	34'
					250 - 225					
'31	25	19	13	6	○	6	13	19	25	31'
					225 - 200					
'28	23	17	11	6	○	6	11	17	23	28'
					200 - 180					
'25	20	15	10	5	○	5	10	15	20	25'

IRON GAME

		LEFT						RIGHT		
					180 - 160					
'15	12	8	6	3	○	3	6	8	12	15'
					160 - 150					
'14	11	8	6	3	○	3	6	8	11	14'
					150 - 140					
'13	10	8	5	3	○	3	5	8	10	13'
					140 - 130					
'11	9	7	5	2	○	2	5	7	9	11'
					130 - 120					
'10	8	6	4	2	○	2	4	6	8	10'

WEDGE GAME

		SHORT						LONG		
					120 - 110					
'15	12	8	6	3	○	3	6	8	12	15'
					110 - 100					
'14	11	8	6	3	○	3	6	8	11	14'
					100 - 90					
'13	10	8	5	3	○	3	5	8	10	13'
					90 - 80					
'11	9	7	5	2	○	2	5	7	9	11'
					80 - 70					
'10	8	6	4	2	○	2	4	6	8	10'
					70 - 60					
'9	7	5	4	2	○	2	4	5	7	9'
					60 - 50					
'8	6	5	3	2	○	2	3	5	6	8'

NOTES ON PERFORMANCE

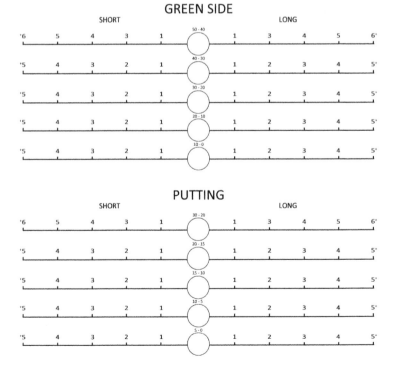

Course: Score: Date:

"The more you praise and celebrate your life, the more there is in life to celebrate."

— OPRAH WINFREY

LONG GAME

LEFT						RIGHT			
				300' - 275					
'38	30	23	15	8	8	15	23	30	38'
				275 - 250					
'34	28	21	14	7	7	14	21	28	34'
				250 - 225					
'31	25	19	13	6	6	13	19	25	31'
				225 - 200					
'28	23	17	11	6	6	11	17	23	28'
				200 - 180					
'25	20	15	10	5	5	10	15	20	25'

IRON GAME

LEFT						RIGHT			
				180 - 160					
'15	12	8	6	3	3	6	8	12	15'
				160 - 150					
'14	11	8	6	3	3	6	8	11	14'
				150 - 140					
'13	10	8	5	3	3	5	8	10	13'
				140 - 130					
'11	9	7	5	2	2	5	7	9	11'
				130 - 120					
'10	8	6	4	2	2	4	6	8	10'

WEDGE GAME

SHORT						LONG			
				120 - 110					
'15	12	8	6	3	3	6	8	12	15'
				110 - 100					
'14	11	8	6	3	3	6	8	11	14'
				100 - 90					
'13	10	8	5	3	3	5	8	10	13'
				90 - 80					
'11	9	7	5	2	2	5	7	9	11'
				80 - 70					
'10	8	6	4	2	2	4	6	8	10'
				70 - 60					
'9	7	5	4	2	2	4	5	7	9'
				60 - 50					
'8	6	5	3	2	2	3	5	6	8'

NOTES ON PERFORMANCE

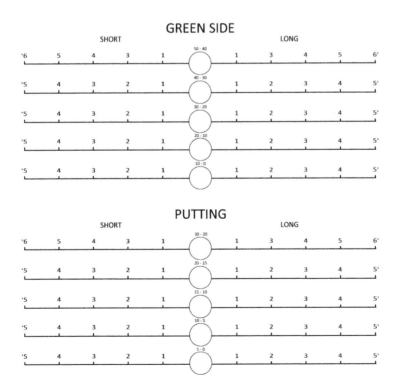

Course: _____ Score: _____ Date: _____

"The most difficult thing is the decision to act, the rest is merely tenacity."

- AMELIA EARHART

LONG GAME

LEFT								RIGHT	
'38	30	23	15	8	300' - 275	8	15	23	30	38'
'34	28	21	14	7	275 - 250	7	14	21	28	34'
'31	25	19	13	6	250 - 225	6	13	19	25	31'
'28	23	17	11	6	225 - 200	6	11	17	23	28'
'25	20	15	10	5	200 - 180	5	10	15	20	25'

IRON GAME

LEFT								RIGHT	
'15	12	8	6	3	180 - 160	3	6	8	12	15'
'14	11	8	6	3	160 - 150	3	6	8	11	14'
'13	10	8	5	3	150 - 140	3	5	8	10	13'
'11	9	7	5	2	140 - 130	2	5	7	9	11'
'10	8	6	4	2	130 - 120	2	4	6	8	10'

WEDGE GAME

SHORT								LONG	
'15	12	8	6	3	120 - 110	3	6	8	12	15'
'14	11	8	6	3	110 - 100	3	6	8	11	14'
'13	10	8	5	3	100 - 90	3	5	8	10	13'
'11	9	7	5	2	90 - 80	2	5	7	9	11'
'10	8	6	4	2	80 - 70	2	4	6	8	10'
'9	7	5	4	2	70 - 60	2	4	5	7	9'
'8	6	5	3	2	60 - 50	2	3	5	6	8'

NOTES ON PERFORMANCE

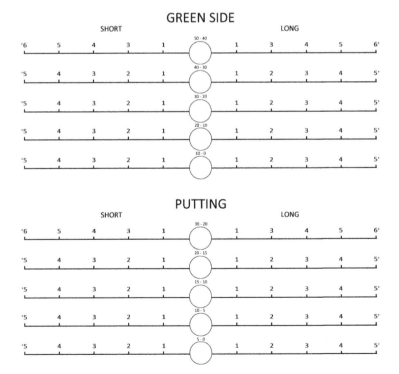

Course: Score: Date:

"All life is an experiment. The more experiments you make the better."

- RALPH WALDO EMERSON

LONG GAME

LEFT						RIGHT			
'38	30	23	15	8	300⁺ - 275	8	15	23	30	38'
'34	28	21	14	7	275 - 250	7	14	21	28	34'
'31	25	19	13	6	250 - 225	6	13	19	25	31'
'28	23	17	11	6	225 - 200	6	11	17	23	28'
'25	20	15	10	5	200 - 180	5	10	15	20	25'

IRON GAME

LEFT						RIGHT			
'15	12	8	6	3	180 - 160	3	6	8	12	15'
'14	11	8	6	3	160 - 150	3	6	8	11	14'
'13	10	8	5	3	150 - 140	3	5	8	10	13'
'11	9	7	5	2	140 - 130	2	5	7	9	11'
'10	8	6	4	2	130 - 120	2	4	6	8	10'

WEDGE GAME

SHORT						LONG			
'15	12	8	6	3	120 - 110	3	6	8	12	15'
'14	11	8	6	3	110 - 100	3	6	8	11	14'
'13	10	8	5	3	100 - 90	3	5	8	10	13'
'11	9	7	5	2	90 - 80	2	5	7	9	11'
'10	8	6	4	2	80 - 70	2	4	6	8	10'
'9	7	5	4	2	70 - 60	2	4	5	7	9'
'8	6	5	3	2	60 - 50	2	3	5	6	8'

NOTES ON PERFORMANCE

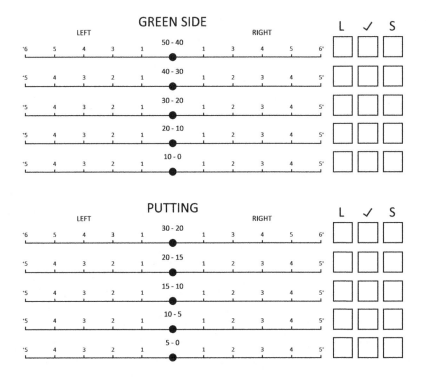

DISPERSION PERFORMANCE REVIEW

"Obstacles are those frightful things you see when you take your eyes off your goal."
HENRY FORD

Which 20% of my yardages are resulting in 80% of my **DISPERSION** from the hole?

1) _____

2) _____

3) _____

4) _____

5) _____

What specific drills can I implement, test and work on to improve on the above?

_____

_____

_____

_____

PROXIMITY PERFORMANCE REVIEW

"If you are honest, truthful, and transparent, people trust you. If people trust you, you have no grounds for fear, suspicion or jealousy."
DALAI LAMA

Which 20% of my yardages are resulting in 80% of my **PROXIMITY** from the hole?

1) _____

2) _____

3) _____

4) _____

5) _____

What specific drills can I implement, test and work on to improve on the above?

_____

_____

_____

_____

Course: _____ Score: _____ Date: _____

"Life doesn't require that we be the best, only that we try our best."

— JACKSON BROWN JR.

LONG GAME

LEFT					300' - 275			RIGHT		
'38	30	23	15	8	○	8	15	23	30	38'
					275 - 250					
'34	28	21	14	7	○	7	14	21	28	34'
					250 - 225					
'31	25	19	13	6	○	6	13	19	25	31'
					225 - 200					
'28	23	17	11	6	○	6	11	17	23	28'
					200 - 180					
'25	20	15	10	5	○	5	10	15	20	25'

IRON GAME

LEFT					180 - 160			RIGHT		
'15	12	8	6	3	○	3	6	8	12	15'
					160 - 150					
'14	11	8	6	3	○	3	6	8	11	14'
					150 - 140					
'13	10	8	5	3	○	3	5	8	10	13'
					140 - 130					
'11	9	7	5	2	○	2	5	7	9	11'
					130 - 120					
'10	8	6	4	2	○	2	4	6	8	10'

WEDGE GAME

SHORT					120 - 110			LONG		
'15	12	8	6	3	○	3	6	8	12	15'
					110 - 100					
'14	11	8	6	3	○	3	6	8	11	14'
					100 - 90					
'13	10	8	5	3	○	3	5	8	10	13'
					90 - 80					
'11	9	7	5	2	○	2	5	7	9	11'
					80 - 70					
'10	8	6	4	2	○	2	4	6	8	10'
					70 - 60					
'9	7	5	4	2	○	2	4	5	7	9'
					60 - 50					
'8	6	5	3	2	○	2	3	5	6	8'

NOTES ON PERFORMANCE

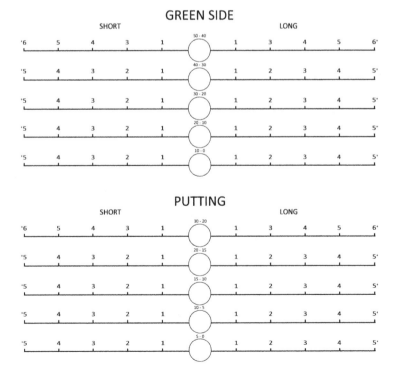

Course: _____ Score: _____ Date: _____

"There is no elevator to success — you have to take the stairs."

— ANONYMOUS

LONG GAME

		LEFT						RIGHT		
'38	30	23	15	8	300'–275	8	15	23	30	38'
'34	28	21	14	7	275–250	7	14	21	28	34'
'31	25	19	13	6	250–225	6	13	19	25	31'
'28	23	17	11	6	225–200	6	11	17	23	28'
'25	20	15	10	5	200–180	5	10	15	20	25'

IRON GAME

		LEFT						RIGHT		
'15	12	8	6	3	180–160	3	6	8	12	15'
'14	11	8	6	3	160–150	3	6	8	11	14'
'13	10	8	5	3	150–140	3	5	8	10	13'
'11	9	7	5	2	140–130	2	5	7	9	11'
'10	8	6	4	2	130–120	2	4	6	8	10'

WEDGE GAME

		SHORT						LONG		
'15	12	8	6	3	120–110	3	6	8	12	15'
'14	11	8	6	3	110–100	3	6	8	11	14'
'13	10	8	5	3	100–90	3	5	8	10	13'
'11	9	7	5	2	90–80	2	5	7	9	11'
'10	8	6	4	2	80–70	2	4	6	8	10'
'9	7	5	4	2	70–60	2	4	5	7	9'
'8	6	5	3	2	60–50	2	3	5	6	8'

NOTES ON PERFORMANCE

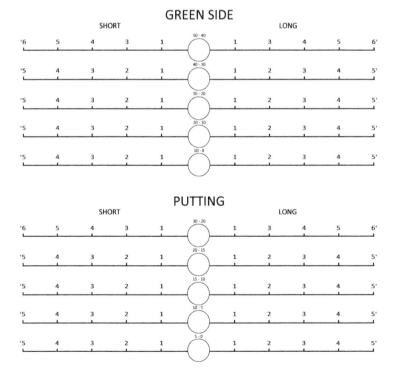

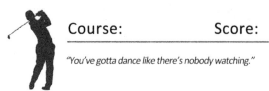

Course: Score: Date:

"You've gotta dance like there's nobody watching."

- WILLIAM W. PURKEY

LONG GAME

LEFT					300'-275		RIGHT			
'38	30	23	15	8	○	8	15	23	30	38'
					275-250					
'34	28	21	14	7	○	7	14	21	28	34'
					250-225					
'31	25	19	13	6	○	6	13	19	25	31'
					225-200					
'28	23	17	11	6	○	6	11	17	23	28'
					200-180					
'25	20	15	10	5	○	5	10	15	20	25'

IRON GAME

LEFT					180-160		RIGHT			
'15	12	8	6	3	○	3	6	8	12	15'
					160-150					
'14	11	8	6	3	○	3	6	8	11	14'
					150-140					
'13	10	8	5	3	○	3	5	8	10	13'
					140-130					
'11	9	7	5	2	○	2	5	7	9	11'
					130-120					
'10	8	6	4	2	○	2	4	6	8	10'

WEDGE GAME

SHORT					120-110		LONG			
'15	12	8	6	3	○	3	6	8	12	15'
					110-100					
'14	11	8	6	3	○	3	6	8	11	14'
					100-90					
'13	10	8	5	3	○	3	5	8	10	13'
					90-80					
'11	9	7	5	2	○	2	5	7	9	11'
					80-70					
'10	8	6	4	2	○	2	4	6	8	10'
					70-60					
'9	7	5	4	2	○	2	4	5	7	9'
					60-50					
'8	6	5	3	2	○	2	3	5	6	8'

NOTES ON PERFORMANCE

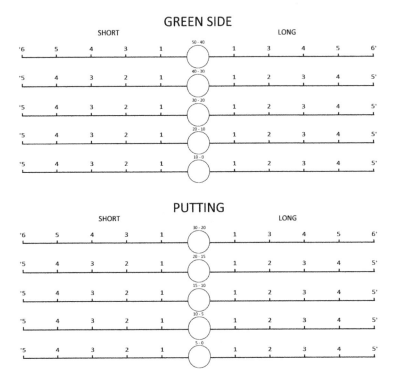

Course: _____ Score: _____ Date: _____

"If you don't pay appropriate attention to what has your attention, it will take more of your attention than it deserves."

— DAVID ALLEN

LONG GAME

LEFT						RIGHT			
					300' - 275				
'38	30	23	15	8	○	8	15	23	30	38'
					275 - 250				
'34	28	21	14	7	○	7	14	21	28	34'
					250 - 225				
'31	25	19	13	6	○	6	13	19	25	31'
					225 - 200				
'28	23	17	11	6	○	6	11	17	23	28'
					200 - 180				
'25	20	15	10	5	○	5	10	15	20	25'

IRON GAME

LEFT						RIGHT			
					180 - 160				
'15	12	8	6	3	○	3	6	8	12	15'
					160 - 150				
'14	11	8	6	3	○	3	6	8	11	14'
					150 - 140				
'13	10	8	5	3	○	3	5	8	10	13'
					140 - 130				
'11	9	7	5	2	○	2	5	7	9	11'
					130 - 120				
'10	8	6	4	2	○	2	4	6	8	10'

WEDGE GAME

SHORT						LONG			
					120 - 110				
'15	12	8	6	3	○	3	6	8	12	15'
					110 - 100				
'14	11	8	6	3	○	3	6	8	11	14'
					100 - 90				
'13	10	8	5	3	○	3	5	8	10	13'
					90 - 80				
'11	9	7	5	2	○	2	5	7	9	11'
					80 - 70				
'10	8	6	4	2	○	2	4	6	8	10'
					70 - 60				
'9	7	5	4	2	○	2	4	5	7	9'
					60 - 50				
'8	6	5	3	2	○	2	3	5	6	8'

NOTES ON PERFORMANCE

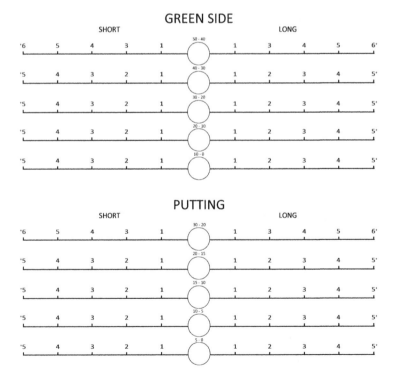

Course: _____ **Score:** _____ **Date:** _____

"Productivity is never an accident. It is always the result of a commitment to excellence, intelligent planning, and focused effort."

— PAUL J. MEYER

LONG GAME

LEFT						RIGHT			
				300⁺ – 275					
'38	30	23	15	8	○	8	15	23	30	38'
				275 – 250					
'34	28	21	14	7	○	7	14	21	28	34'
				250 – 225					
'31	25	19	13	6	○	6	13	19	25	31'
				225 – 200					
'28	23	17	11	6	○	6	11	17	23	28'
				200 – 180					
'25	20	15	10	5	○	5	10	15	20	25'

IRON GAME

LEFT						RIGHT			
				180 – 160					
'15	12	8	6	3	○	3	6	8	12	15'
				160 – 150					
'14	11	8	6	3	○	3	6	8	11	14'
				150 – 140					
'13	10	8	5	3	○	3	5	8	10	13'
				140 – 130					
'11	9	7	5	2	○	2	5	7	9	11'
				130 – 120					
'10	8	6	4	2	○	2	4	6	8	10'

WEDGE GAME

SHORT						LONG			
				120 – 110					
'15	12	8	6	3	○	3	6	8	12	15'
				110 – 100					
'14	11	8	6	3	○	3	6	8	11	14'
				100 – 90					
'13	10	8	5	3	○	3	5	8	10	13'
				90 – 80					
'11	9	7	5	2	○	2	5	7	9	11'
				80 – 70					
'10	8	6	4	2	○	2	4	6	8	10'
				70 – 60					
'9	7	5	4	2	○	2	4	5	7	9'
				60 – 50					
'8	6	5	3	2	○	2	3	5	6	8'

NOTES ON PERFORMANCE

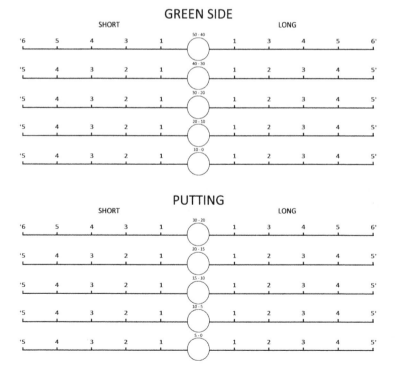

Course: Score: Date:

"You may delay, but time will not."

— BENJAMIN FRANKLIN

LONG GAME

LEFT					RIGHT			
'38	30	23	15	8 — 300'-275 — 8	15	23	30	38'
'34	28	21	14	7 — 275-250 — 7	14	21	28	34'
'31	25	19	13	6 — 250-225 — 6	13	19	25	31'
'28	23	17	11	6 — 225-200 — 6	11	17	23	28'
'25	20	15	10	5 — 200-180 — 5	10	15	20	25'

IRON GAME

LEFT					RIGHT			
'15	12	8	6	3 — 180-160 — 3	6	8	12	15'
'14	11	8	6	3 — 160-150 — 3	6	8	11	14'
'13	10	8	5	3 — 150-140 — 3	5	8	10	13'
'11	9	7	5	2 — 140-130 — 2	5	7	9	11'
'10	8	6	4	2 — 130-120 — 2	4	6	8	10'

WEDGE GAME

SHORT					LONG			
'15	12	8	6	3 — 120-110 — 3	6	8	12	15'
'14	11	8	6	3 — 110-100 — 3	6	8	11	14'
'13	10	8	5	3 — 100-90 — 3	5	8	10	13'
'11	9	7	5	2 — 90-80 — 2	5	7	9	11'
'10	8	6	4	2 — 80-70 — 2	4	6	8	10'
'9	7	5	4	2 — 70-60 — 2	4	5	7	9'
'8	6	5	3	2 — 60-50 — 2	3	5	6	8'

NOTES ON PERFORMANCE

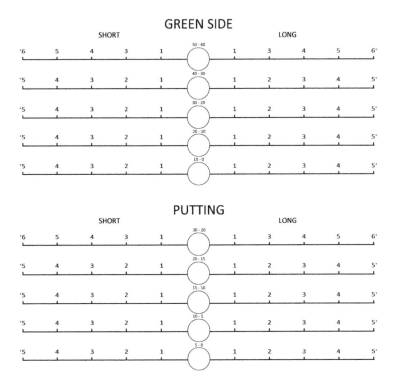

DISPERSION
PERFORMANCE REVIEW

"You see, in life, lots of people know what to do, but few people actually do what they know. Knowing is not enough! You must take action."
TONY ROBBINS

Which 20% of my yardages are resulting in 80% of my **DISPERSION** from the hole?

1) _____

2) _____

3) _____

4) _____

5) _____

What specific drills can I implement, test and work on to improve on the above?

_____

_____

_____

_____

PROXIMITY PERFORMANCE REVIEW

"Remember that failure is an event, not a person."
ZIG ZIGLAR

Which 20% of my yardages are resulting in 80% of my **PROXIMITY** from the hole?

1) _____

2) _____

3) _____

4) _____

5) _____

What specific drills can I implement, test and work on to improve on the above?

_____

_____

_____

_____

Course: _____ Score: _____ Date: _____

"The best way out is always through."

- ROBERT FROST

LONG GAME

		LEFT			300'- 275			RIGHT		
'38	30	23	15	8	○	8	15	23	30	38'
					275 - 250					
'34	28	21	14	7	○	7	14	21	28	34'
					250 - 225					
'31	25	19	13	6	○	6	13	19	25	31'
					225 - 200					
'28	23	17	11	6	○	6	11	17	23	28'
					200 - 180					
'25	20	15	10	5	○	5	10	15	20	25'

IRON GAME

		LEFT			180 - 160			RIGHT		
'15	12	8	6	3	○	3	6	8	12	15'
					160 - 150					
'14	11	8	6	3	○	3	6	8	11	14'
					150 - 140					
'13	10	8	5	3	○	3	5	8	10	13'
					140 - 130					
'11	9	7	5	2	○	2	5	7	9	11'
					130 - 120					
'10	8	6	4	2	○	2	4	6	8	10'

WEDGE GAME

		SHORT			120 - 110			LONG		
'15	12	8	6	3	○	3	6	8	12	15'
					110 - 100					
'14	11	8	6	3	○	3	6	8	11	14'
					100 - 90					
'13	10	8	5	3	○	3	5	8	10	13'
					90 - 80					
'11	9	7	5	2	○	2	5	7	9	11'
					80 - 70					
'10	8	6	4	2	○	2	4	6	8	10'
					70 - 60					
'9	7	5	4	2	○	2	4	5	7	9'
					60 - 50					
'8	6	5	3	2	○	2	3	5	6	8'

NOTES ON PERFORMANCE

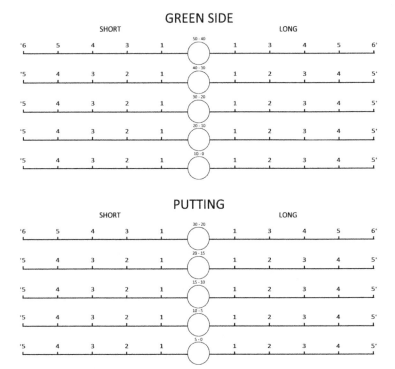

Course: Score: Date:

"If there are nine rabbits on the ground, if you want to catch one, just focus on one."

                                                            - JACK MA

LONG GAME

LEFT						RIGHT			
				300' - 275					
'38	30	23	15	8	8	15	23	30	38'
				275 - 250					
'34	28	21	14	7	7	14	21	28	34'
				250 - 225					
'31	25	19	13	6	6	13	19	25	31'
				225 - 200					
'28	23	17	11	6	6	11	17	23	28'
				200 - 180					
'25	20	15	10	5	5	10	15	20	25'

IRON GAME

LEFT						RIGHT			
				180 - 160					
'15	12	8	6	3	3	6	8	12	15'
				160 - 150					
'14	11	8	6	3	3	6	8	11	14'
				150 - 140					
'13	10	8	5	3	3	5	8	10	13'
				140 - 130					
'11	9	7	5	2	2	5	7	9	11'
				130 - 120					
'10	8	6	4	2	2	4	6	8	10'

WEDGE GAME

SHORT						LONG			
				120 - 110					
'15	12	8	6	3	3	6	8	12	15'
				110 - 100					
'14	11	8	6	3	3	6	8	11	14'
				100 - 90					
'13	10	8	5	3	3	5	8	10	13'
				90 - 80					
'11	9	7	5	2	2	5	7	9	11'
				80 - 70					
'10	8	6	4	2	2	4	6	8	10'
				70 - 60					
'9	7	5	4	2	2	4	5	7	9'
				60 - 50					
'8	6	5	3	2	2	3	5	6	8'

NOTES ON PERFORMANCE

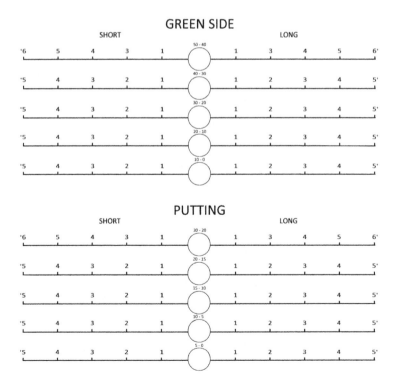

Course: _____ Score: _____ Date: _____

"Whatever the mind of man can conceive and believe, it can achieve. Thoughts are things!"

- NAPOLEON HILL

LONG GAME

LEFT						RIGHT			
'38	30	23	15	8	**300'-275**	8	15	23	30	38'
'34	28	21	14	7	**275-250**	7	14	21	28	34'
'31	25	19	13	6	**250-225**	6	13	19	25	31'
'28	23	17	11	6	**225-200**	6	11	17	23	28'
'25	20	15	10	5	**200-180**	5	10	15	20	25'

IRON GAME

LEFT						RIGHT			
'15	12	8	6	3	**180-160**	3	6	8	12	15'
'14	11	8	6	3	**160-150**	3	6	8	11	14'
'13	10	8	5	3	**150-140**	3	5	8	10	13'
'11	9	7	5	2	**140-130**	2	5	7	9	11'
'10	8	6	4	2	**130-120**	2	4	6	8	10'

WEDGE GAME

SHORT						LONG			
'15	12	8	6	3	**120-110**	3	6	8	12	15'
'14	11	8	6	3	**110-100**	3	6	8	11	14'
'13	10	8	5	3	**100-90**	3	5	8	10	13'
'11	9	7	5	2	**90-80**	2	5	7	9	11'
'10	8	6	4	2	**80-70**	2	4	6	8	10'
'9	7	5	4	2	**70-60**	2	4	5	7	9'
'8	6	5	3	2	**60-50**	2	3	5	6	8'

NOTES ON PERFORMANCE

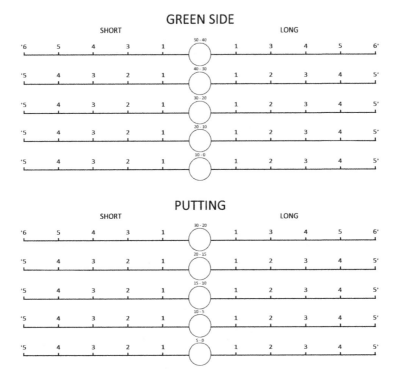

Course: _____ Score: _____ Date: _____

"A life spent making mistakes is not only more honorable, but more useful than a life spent doing nothing"

- GEORGE BERNARD SHAW

LONG GAME

LEFT						RIGHT			
				300' - 275					
'38	30	23	15	8	8	15	23	30	38'
				275 - 250					
'34	28	21	14	7	7	14	21	28	34'
				250 - 225					
'31	25	19	13	6	6	13	19	25	31'
				225 - 200					
'28	23	17	11	6	6	11	17	23	28'
				200 - 180					
'25	20	15	10	5	5	10	15	20	25'

IRON GAME

LEFT						RIGHT			
				180 - 160					
'15	12	8	6	3	3	6	8	12	15'
				160 - 150					
'14	11	8	6	3	3	6	8	11	14'
				150 - 140					
'13	10	8	5	3	3	5	8	10	13'
				140 - 130					
'11	9	7	5	2	2	5	7	9	11'
				130 - 120					
'10	8	6	4	2	2	4	6	8	10'

WEDGE GAME

SHORT						LONG			
				120 - 110					
'15	12	8	6	3	3	6	8	12	15'
				110 - 100					
'14	11	8	6	3	3	6	8	11	14'
				100 - 90					
'13	10	8	5	3	3	5	8	10	13'
				90 - 80					
'11	9	7	5	2	2	5	7	9	11'
				80 - 70					
'10	8	6	4	2	2	4	6	8	10'
				70 - 60					
'9	7	5	4	2	2	4	5	7	9'
				60 - 50					
'8	6	5	3	2	2	3	5	6	8'

NOTES ON PERFORMANCE

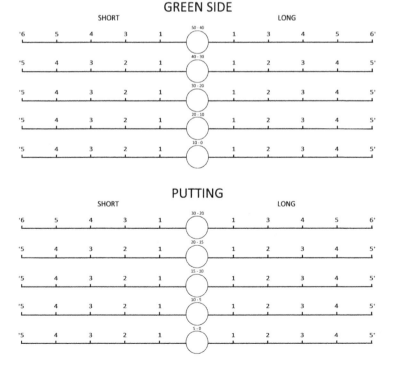

Course: _____ Score: _____ Date: _____

"Focus on being productive instead of busy."

- TIM FERRISS

LONG GAME

		LEFT					RIGHT		
					300' - 275				
'38	30	23	15	8		8	15	23	30	38'
					275 - 250				
'34	28	21	14	7		7	14	21	28	34'
					250 - 225				
'31	25	19	13	6		6	13	19	25	31'
					225 - 200				
'28	23	17	11	6		6	11	17	23	28'
					200 - 180				
'25	20	15	10	5		5	10	15	20	25'

IRON GAME

		LEFT					RIGHT		
					180 - 160				
'15	12	8	6	3		3	6	8	12	15'
					160 - 150				
'14	11	8	6	3		3	6	8	11	14'
					150 - 140				
'13	10	8	5	3		3	5	8	10	13'
					140 - 130				
'11	9	7	5	2		2	5	7	9	11'
					130 - 120				
'10	8	6	4	2		2	4	6	8	10'

WEDGE GAME

		SHORT					LONG		
					120 - 110				
'15	12	8	6	3		3	6	8	12	15'
					110 - 100				
'14	11	8	6	3		3	6	8	11	14'
					100 - 90				
'13	10	8	5	3		3	5	8	10	13'
					90 - 80				
'11	9	7	5	2		2	5	7	9	11'
					80 - 70				
'10	8	6	4	2		2	4	6	8	10'
					70 - 60				
'9	7	5	4	2		2	4	5	7	9'
					60 - 50				
'8	6	5	3	2		2	3	5	6	8'

NOTES ON PERFORMANCE

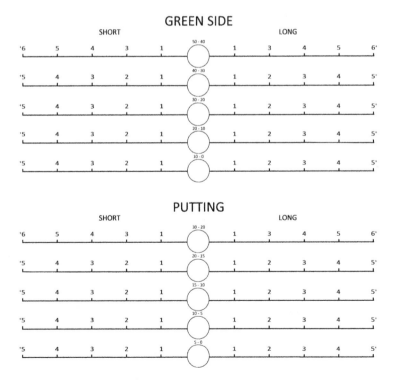

Course: _____   Score: _____   Date: _____

"When you've got something to prove, there's nothing greater than a challenge."

- TERRY BRADSHAW

LONG GAME

LEFT						RIGHT			
'38	30	23	15	8	300⁺ - 275 ○ 8	15	23	30	38'
'34	28	21	14	7	275 - 250 ○ 7	14	21	28	34'
'31	25	19	13	6	250 - 225 ○ 6	13	19	25	31'
'28	23	17	11	6	225 - 200 ○ 6	11	17	23	28'
'25	20	15	10	5	200 - 180 ○ 5	10	15	20	25'

IRON GAME

LEFT						RIGHT			
'15	12	8	6	3	180 - 160 ○ 3	6	8	12	15'
'14	11	8	6	3	160 - 150 ○ 3	6	8	11	14'
'13	10	8	5	3	150 - 140 ○ 3	5	8	10	13'
'11	9	7	5	2	140 - 130 ○ 2	5	7	9	11'
'10	8	6	4	2	130 - 120 ○ 2	4	6	8	10'

WEDGE GAME

SHORT						LONG			
'15	12	8	6	3	120 - 110 ○ 3	6	8	12	15'
'14	11	8	6	3	110 - 100 ○ 3	6	8	11	14'
'13	10	8	5	3	100 - 90 ○ 3	5	8	10	13'
'11	9	7	5	2	90 - 80 ○ 2	5	7	9	11'
'10	8	6	4	2	80 - 70 ○ 2	4	6	8	10'
'9	7	5	4	2	70 - 60 ○ 2	4	5	7	9'
'8	6	5	3	2	60 - 50 ○ 2	3	5	6	8'

NOTES ON PERFORMANCE

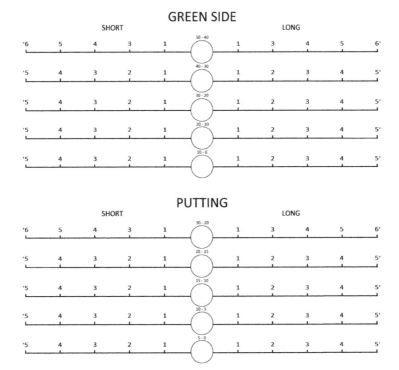

DISPERSION PERFORMANCE REVIEW

"We have a strategic plan. It's called doing things."
HERB KELLEHER

Which 20% of my yardages are resulting in 80% of my **DISPERSION** from the hole?

1) _____

2) _____

3) _____

4) _____

5) _____

What specific drills can I implement, test and work on to improve on the above?

_____

_____

_____

_____

PROXIMITY PERFORMANCE REVIEW

"Think of many things; do one."
PORTUGUESE PROVERB

Which 20% of my yardages are resulting in 80% of my **PROXIMITY** from the hole?

1) _____
2) _____
3) _____
4) _____
5) _____

What specific drills can I implement, test and work on to improve on the above?

_____
_____
_____
_____

Course: Score: Date:

"You don't need a new plan for next year. You need a commitment."

— SETH GODIN

LONG GAME

LEFT							RIGHT		
'38	30	23	15	8	300' – 275 ○ 8	15	23	30	38'
'34	28	21	14	7	275 – 250 ○ 7	14	21	28	34'
'31	25	19	13	6	250 – 225 ○ 6	13	19	25	31'
'28	23	17	11	6	225 – 200 ○ 6	11	17	23	28'
'25	20	15	10	5	200 – 180 ○ 5	10	15	20	25'

IRON GAME

LEFT							RIGHT		
'15	12	8	6	3	180 – 160 ○ 3	6	8	12	15'
'14	11	8	6	3	160 – 150 ○ 3	6	8	11	14'
'13	10	8	5	3	150 – 140 ○ 3	5	8	10	13'
'11	9	7	5	2	140 – 130 ○ 2	5	7	9	11'
'10	8	6	4	2	130 – 120 ○ 2	4	6	8	10'

WEDGE GAME

SHORT							LONG		
'15	12	8	6	3	120 – 110 ○ 3	6	8	12	15'
'14	11	8	6	3	110 – 100 ○ 3	6	8	11	14'
'13	10	8	5	3	100 – 90 ○ 3	5	8	10	13'
'11	9	7	5	2	90 – 80 ○ 2	5	7	9	11'
'10	8	6	4	2	80 – 70 ○ 2	4	6	8	10'
'9	7	5	4	2	70 – 60 ○ 2	4	5	7	9'
'8	6	5	3	2	60 – 50 ○ 2	3	5	6	8'

NOTES ON PERFORMANCE

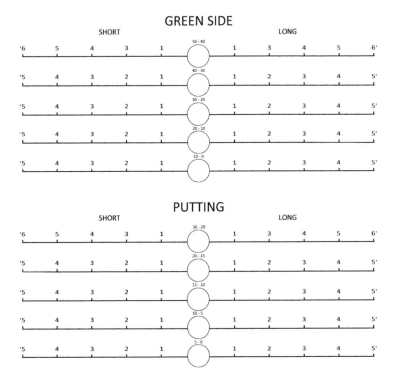

Course: _____ Score: _____ Date: _____

"Lost time is never found again."

— BENJAMIN FRANKLIN

LONG GAME

LEFT								RIGHT	
					300⁺ - 275				
'38	30	23	15	8	○	8	15	23	30	38⁺
					275 - 250				
'34	28	21	14	7	○	7	14	21	28	34⁺
					250 - 225				
'31	25	19	13	6	○	6	13	19	25	31⁺
					225 - 200				
'28	23	17	11	6	○	6	11	17	23	28⁺
					200 - 180				
'25	20	15	10	5	○	5	10	15	20	25⁺

IRON GAME

LEFT								RIGHT	
					180 - 160				
'15	12	8	6	3	○	3	6	8	12	15⁺
					160 - 150				
'14	11	8	6	3	○	3	6	8	11	14⁺
					150 - 140				
'13	10	8	5	3	○	3	5	8	10	13⁺
					140 - 130				
'11	9	7	5	2	○	2	5	7	9	11⁺
					130 - 120				
'10	8	6	4	2	○	2	4	6	8	10⁺

WEDGE GAME

SHORT								LONG	
					120 - 110				
'15	12	8	6	3	○	3	6	8	12	15⁺
					110 - 100				
'14	11	8	6	3	○	3	6	8	11	14⁺
					100 - 90				
'13	10	8	5	3	○	3	5	8	10	13⁺
					90 - 80				
'11	9	7	5	2	○	2	5	7	9	11⁺
					80 - 70				
'10	8	6	4	2	○	2	4	6	8	10⁺
					70 - 60				
'9	7	5	4	2	○	2	4	5	7	9⁺
					60 - 50				
'8	6	5	3	2	○	2	3	5	6	8⁺

NOTES ON PERFORMANCE

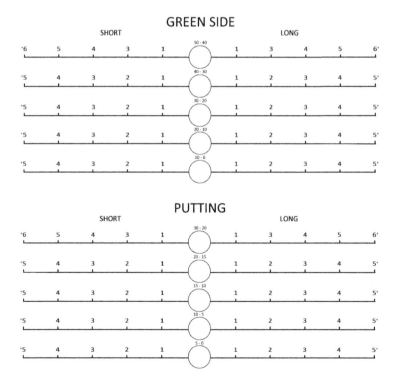

Course: _____ Score: _____ Date: _____

"Don't confuse the urgent with the important."

— PRESTON NI

LONG GAME

LEFT				300'-275				RIGHT
'38	30	23	15	8 ○ 8	15	23	30	38'
'34	28	21	14	7 ○ 7	14	21	28	34'
				275-250				
'31	25	19	13	6 ○ 6	13	19	25	31'
				250-225				
'28	23	17	11	6 ○ 6	11	17	23	28'
				225-200				
'25	20	15	10	5 ○ 5	10	15	20	25'
				200-180				

IRON GAME

LEFT				180-160				RIGHT
'15	12	8	6	3 ○ 3	6	8	12	15'
'14	11	8	6	3 ○ 3	6	8	11	14'
				160-150				
'13	10	8	5	3 ○ 3	5	8	10	13'
				150-140				
'11	9	7	5	2 ○ 2	5	7	9	11'
				140-130				
'10	8	6	4	2 ○ 2	4	6	8	10'
				130-120				

WEDGE GAME

SHORT				120-110				LONG
'15	12	8	6	3 ○ 3	6	8	12	15'
'14	11	8	6	3 ○ 3	6	8	11	14'
				110-100				
'13	10	8	5	3 ○ 3	5	8	10	13'
				100-90				
'11	9	7	5	2 ○ 2	5	7	9	11'
				90-80				
'10	8	6	4	2 ○ 2	4	6	8	10'
				80-70				
'9	7	5	4	2 ○ 2	4	5	7	9'
				70-60				
'8	6	5	3	2 ○ 2	3	5	6	8'
				60-50				

NOTES ON PERFORMANCE

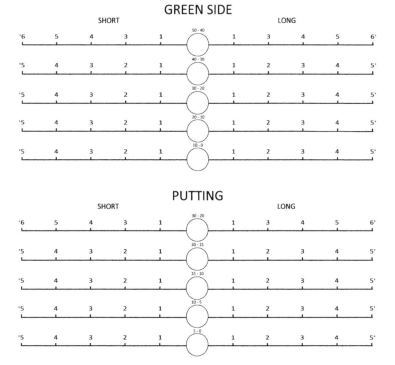

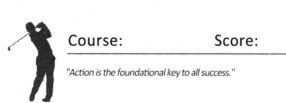

Course: _____ Score: _____ Date: _____

"Action is the foundational key to all success."

- PABLO PICASSO

LONG GAME

LEFT						RIGHT			
				300+ - 275					
'38	30	23	15	8	8	15	23	30	38'
				275 - 250					
'34	28	21	14	7	7	14	21	28	34'
				250 - 225					
'31	25	19	13	6	6	13	19	25	31'
				225 - 200					
'28	23	17	11	6	6	11	17	23	28'
				200 - 180					
'25	20	15	10	5	5	10	15	20	25'

IRON GAME

LEFT						RIGHT			
				180 - 160					
'15	12	8	6	3	3	6	8	12	15'
				160 - 150					
'14	11	8	6	3	3	6	8	11	14'
				150 - 140					
'13	10	8	5	3	3	5	8	10	13'
				140 - 130					
'11	9	7	5	2	2	5	7	9	11'
				130 - 120					
'10	8	6	4	2	2	4	6	8	10'

WEDGE GAME

SHORT						LONG			
				120 - 110					
'15	12	8	6	3	3	6	8	12	15'
				110 - 100					
'14	11	8	6	3	3	6	8	11	14'
				100 - 90					
'13	10	8	5	3	3	5	8	10	13'
				90 - 80					
'11	9	7	5	2	2	5	7	9	11'
				80 - 70					
'10	8	6	4	2	2	4	6	8	10'
				70 - 60					
'9	7	5	4	2	2	4	5	7	9'
				60 - 50					
'8	6	5	3	2	2	3	5	6	8'

NOTES ON PERFORMANCE

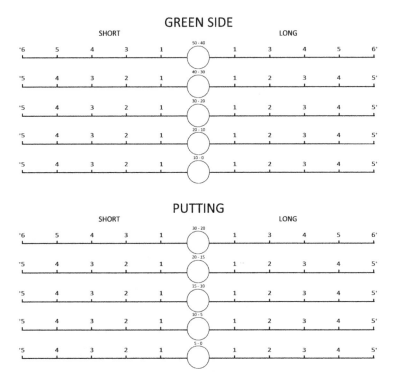

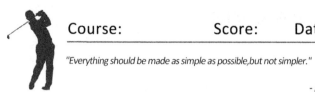

Course: _____ Score: _____ Date: _____

"Everything should be made as simple as possible, but not simpler."

- ALBERT EINSTEIN

LONG GAME

LEFT						RIGHT			
'38	30	23	15	8	**300⁺ - 275**	8	15	23	30	38'
'34	28	21	14	7	**275 - 250**	7	14	21	28	34'
'31	25	19	13	6	**250 - 225**	6	13	19	25	31'
'28	23	17	11	6	**225 - 200**	6	11	17	23	28'
'25	20	15	10	5	**200 - 180**	5	10	15	20	25'

IRON GAME

LEFT						RIGHT			
'15	12	8	6	3	**180 - 160**	3	6	8	12	15'
'14	11	8	6	3	**160 - 150**	3	6	8	11	14'
'13	10	8	5	3	**150 - 140**	3	5	8	10	13'
'11	9	7	5	2	**140 - 130**	2	5	7	9	11'
'10	8	6	4	2	**130 - 120**	2	4	6	8	10'

WEDGE GAME

SHORT						LONG			
'15	12	8	6	3	**120 - 110**	3	6	8	12	15'
'14	11	8	6	3	**110 - 100**	3	6	8	11	14'
'13	10	8	5	3	**100 - 90**	3	5	8	10	13'
'11	9	7	5	2	**90 - 80**	2	5	7	9	11'
'10	8	6	4	2	**80 - 70**	2	4	6	8	10'
'9	7	5	4	2	**70 - 60**	2	4	5	7	9'
'8	6	5	3	2	**60 - 50**	2	3	5	6	8'

NOTES ON PERFORMANCE

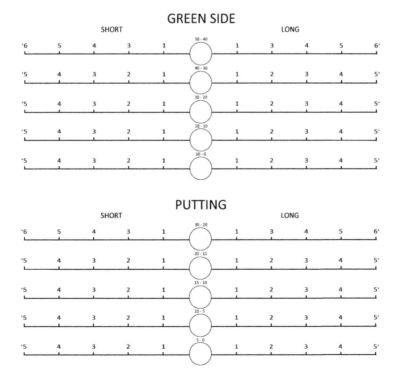

Course: _____ Score: _____ Date: _____

"Motivation is what gets you started. Habit is what keeps you going."

- JIM RYUN

LONG GAME

LEFT						RIGHT			
'38	30	23	15	8	300⁺ - 275	8	15	23	30	38'
'34	28	21	14	7	275 - 250	7	14	21	28	34'
'31	25	19	13	6	250 - 225	6	13	19	25	31'
'28	23	17	11	6	225 - 200	6	11	17	23	28'
'25	20	15	10	5	200 - 180	5	10	15	20	25'

IRON GAME

LEFT						RIGHT			
'15	12	8	6	3	180 - 160	3	6	8	12	15'
'14	11	8	6	3	160 - 150	3	6	8	11	14'
'13	10	8	5	3	150 - 140	3	5	8	10	13'
'11	9	7	5	2	140 - 130	2	5	7	9	11'
'10	8	6	4	2	130 - 120	2	4	6	8	10'

WEDGE GAME

SHORT						LONG			
'15	12	8	6	3	120 - 110	3	6	8	12	15'
'14	11	8	6	3	110 - 100	3	6	8	11	14'
'13	10	8	5	3	100 - 90	3	5	8	10	13'
'11	9	7	5	2	90 - 80	2	5	7	9	11'
'10	8	6	4	2	80 - 70	2	4	6	8	10'
'9	7	5	4	2	70 - 60	2	4	5	7	9'
'8	6	5	3	2	60 - 50	2	3	5	6	8'

NOTES ON PERFORMANCE

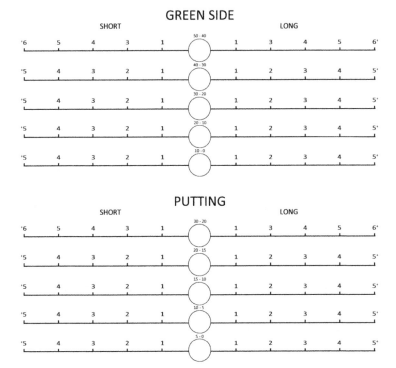

DISPERSION
PERFORMANCE REVIEW

"If you spend too much time thinking about a thing, you'll never get it done."
BRUCE LEE

Which 20% of my yardages are resulting in 80% of my **DISPERSION** from the hole?

1) _____

2) _____

3) _____

4) _____

5) _____

What specific drills can I implement, test and work on to improve on the above?

_____

_____

_____

_____

PROXIMITY PERFORMANCE REVIEW

"Create with the heart; build with the mind."
CRISS JAMI

Which 20% of my yardages are resulting in 80% of my **PROXIMITY** from the hole?

1) _____

2) _____

3) _____

4) _____

5) _____

What specific drills can I implement, test and work on to improve on the above?

_____

_____

_____

_____

Course: _____   Score: _____   Date: _____

"There may be people that have more talent than you, but there's no excuse for anyone to work harder than you do."

- DEREK JETER

LONG GAME

		LEFT					RIGHT			
'38	30	23	15	8	300' - 275	8	15	23	30	38'
'34	28	21	14	7	275 - 250	7	14	21	28	34'
'31	25	19	13	6	250 - 225	6	13	19	25	31'
'28	23	17	11	6	225 - 200	6	11	17	23	28'
'25	20	15	10	5	200 - 180	5	10	15	20	25'

IRON GAME

		LEFT					RIGHT			
'15	12	8	6	3	180 - 160	3	6	8	12	15'
'14	11	8	6	3	160 - 150	3	6	8	11	14'
'13	10	8	5	3	150 - 140	3	5	8	10	13'
'11	9	7	5	2	140 - 130	2	5	7	9	11'
'10	8	6	4	2	130 - 120	2	4	6	8	10'

WEDGE GAME

		SHORT					LONG			
'15	12	8	6	3	120 - 110	3	6	8	12	15'
'14	11	8	6	3	110 - 100	3	6	8	11	14'
'13	10	8	5	3	100 - 90	3	5	8	10	13'
'11	9	7	5	2	90 - 80	2	5	7	9	11'
'10	8	6	4	2	80 - 70	2	4	6	8	10'
'9	7	5	4	2	70 - 60	2	4	5	7	9'
'8	6	5	3	2	60 - 50	2	3	5	6	8'

NOTES ON PERFORMANCE

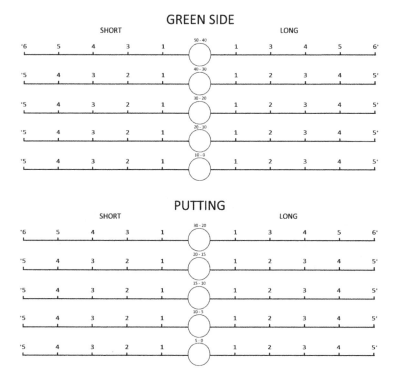

Course: _____ Score: _____ Date: _____

"One man practicing sportsmanship is far better than 50 preaching it."

— KNUTE ROCKNE

LONG GAME

LEFT				300⁺ - 275				RIGHT
'38	30	23	15	8 ◯ 8	15	23	30	38'
'34	28	21	14	7 ◯ 7	14	21	28	34'
'31	25	19	13	6 ◯ 6	13	19	25	31'
'28	23	17	11	6 ◯ 6	11	17	23	28'
'25	20	15	10	5 ◯ 5	10	15	20	25'

(275 - 250, 250 - 225, 225 - 200, 200 - 180)

IRON GAME

LEFT				180 - 160				RIGHT
'15	12	8	6	3 ◯ 3	6	8	12	15'
'14	11	8	6	3 ◯ 3	6	8	11	14'
'13	10	8	5	3 ◯ 3	5	8	10	13'
'11	9	7	5	2 ◯ 2	5	7	9	11'
'10	8	6	4	2 ◯ 2	4	6	8	10'

(160 - 150, 150 - 140, 140 - 130, 130 - 120)

WEDGE GAME

SHORT				120 - 110				LONG
'15	12	8	6	3 ◯ 3	6	8	12	15'
'14	11	8	6	3 ◯ 3	6	8	11	14'
'13	10	8	5	3 ◯ 3	5	8	10	13'
'11	9	7	5	2 ◯ 2	5	7	9	11'
'10	8	6	4	2 ◯ 2	4	6	8	10'
'9	7	5	4	2 ◯ 2	4	5	7	9'
'8	6	5	3	2 ◯ 2	3	5	6	8'

(110 - 100, 100 - 90, 90 - 80, 80 - 70, 70 - 60, 60 - 50)

NOTES ON PERFORMANCE

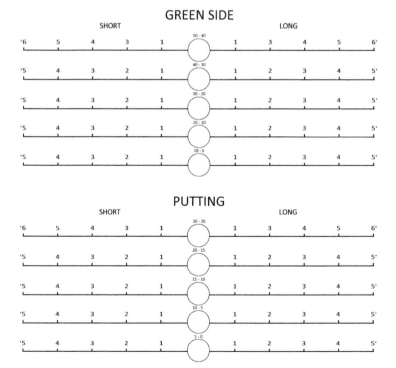

Course: _____   Score: _____   Date: _____

"Do what is right, not what is easy."

- ROY T. BENNETT

LONG GAME

LEFT						RIGHT			
'38	30	23	15	8	**300+ - 275** 8	15	23	30	38'
'34	28	21	14	7	**275 - 250** 7	14	21	28	34'
'31	25	19	13	6	**250 - 225** 6	13	19	25	31'
'28	23	17	11	6	**225 - 200** 6	11	17	23	28'
'25	20	15	10	5	**200 - 180** 5	10	15	20	25'

IRON GAME

LEFT						RIGHT			
'15	12	8	6	3	**180 - 160** 3	6	8	12	15'
'14	11	8	6	3	**160 - 150** 3	6	8	11	14'
'13	10	8	5	3	**150 - 140** 3	5	8	10	13'
'11	9	7	5	2	**140 - 130** 2	5	7	9	11'
'10	8	6	4	2	**130 - 120** 2	4	6	8	10'

WEDGE GAME

SHORT						LONG			
'15	12	8	6	3	**120 - 110** 3	6	8	12	15'
'14	11	8	6	3	**110 - 100** 3	6	8	11	14'
'13	10	8	5	3	**100 - 90** 3	5	8	10	13'
'11	9	7	5	2	**90 - 80** 2	5	7	9	11'
'10	8	6	4	2	**80 - 70** 2	4	6	8	10'
'9	7	5	4	2	**70 - 60** 2	4	5	7	9'
'8	6	5	3	2	**60 - 50** 2	3	5	6	8'

NOTES ON PERFORMANCE

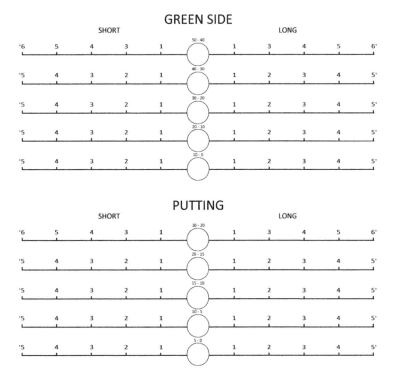

Course: Score: Date:

"And the day came when the risk to remain tight in a bud was more painful than the risk it took to blossom."

— ANAIS NIN

LONG GAME

		LEFT			300'- 275			RIGHT		
'38	30	23	15	8	○	8	15	23	30	38'
'34	28	21	14	7	275 – 250 ○	7	14	21	28	34'
'31	25	19	13	6	250 – 225 ○	6	13	19	25	31'
'28	23	17	11	6	225 – 200 ○	6	11	17	23	28'
'25	20	15	10	5	200 – 180 ○	5	10	15	20	25'

IRON GAME

		LEFT			180 – 160			RIGHT		
'15	12	8	6	3	○	3	6	8	12	15'
'14	11	8	6	3	160 – 150 ○	3	6	8	11	14'
'13	10	8	5	3	150 – 140 ○	3	5	8	10	13'
'11	9	7	5	2	140 – 130 ○	2	5	7	9	11'
'10	8	6	4	2	130 – 120 ○	2	4	6	8	10'

WEDGE GAME

		SHORT			120 – 110			LONG		
'15	12	8	6	3	○	3	6	8	12	15'
'14	11	8	6	3	110 – 100 ○	3	6	8	11	14'
'13	10	8	5	3	100 – 90 ○	3	5	8	10	13'
'11	9	7	5	2	90 – 80 ○	2	5	7	9	11'
'10	8	6	4	2	80 – 70 ○	2	4	6	8	10'
'9	7	5	4	2	70 – 60 ○	2	4	5	7	9'
'8	6	5	3	2	60 – 50 ○	2	3	5	6	8'

NOTES ON PERFORMANCE

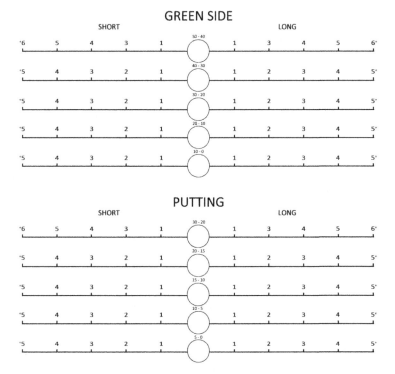

Course: Score: Date:

"Do it right"

- GEORGE GREENBURY

LONG GAME

		LEFT					RIGHT		
'38	30	23	15	8	300' - 275	8	15	23	30	38'
'34	28	21	14	7	275 - 250	7	14	21	28	34'
'31	25	19	13	6	250 - 225	6	13	19	25	31'
'28	23	17	11	6	225 - 200	6	11	17	23	28'
'25	20	15	10	5	200 - 180	5	10	15	20	25'

IRON GAME

		LEFT					RIGHT		
'15	12	8	6	3	180 - 160	3	6	8	12	15'
'14	11	8	6	3	160 - 150	3	6	8	11	14'
'13	10	8	5	3	150 - 140	3	5	8	10	13'
'11	9	7	5	2	140 - 130	2	5	7	9	11'
'10	8	6	4	2	130 - 120	2	4	6	8	10'

WEDGE GAME

		SHORT					LONG		
'15	12	8	6	3	120 - 110	3	6	8	12	15'
'14	11	8	6	3	110 - 100	3	6	8	11	14'
'13	10	8	5	3	100 - 90	3	5	8	10	13'
'11	9	7	5	2	90 - 80	2	5	7	9	11'
'10	8	6	4	2	80 - 70	2	4	6	8	10'
'9	7	5	4	2	70 - 60	2	4	5	7	9'
'8	6	5	3	2	60 - 50	2	3	5	6	8'

NOTES ON PERFORMANCE

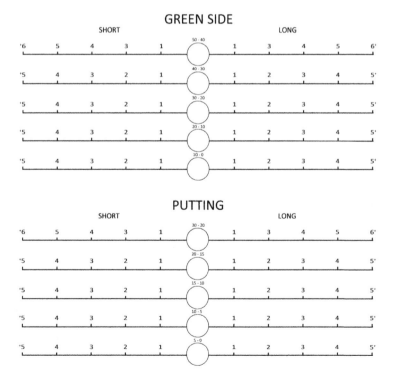

Course: _____ Score: _____ Date: _____

"A year from now you will wish you had started today."

- KAREN LAMB

LONG GAME

LEFT						RIGHT			
'38	30	23	15	8	300'-275	8	15	23	30	38'
'34	28	21	14	7	275-250	7	14	21	28	34'
'31	25	19	13	6	250-225	6	13	19	25	31'
'28	23	17	11	6	225-200	6	11	17	23	28'
'25	20	15	10	5	200-180	5	10	15	20	25'

IRON GAME

LEFT						RIGHT			
'15	12	8	6	3	180-160	3	6	8	12	15'
'14	11	8	6	3	160-150	3	6	8	11	14'
'13	10	8	5	3	150-140	3	5	8	10	13'
'11	9	7	5	2	140-130	2	5	7	9	11'
'10	8	6	4	2	130-120	2	4	6	8	10'

WEDGE GAME

SHORT						LONG			
'15	12	8	6	3	120-110	3	6	8	12	15'
'14	11	8	6	3	110-100	3	6	8	11	14'
'13	10	8	5	3	100-90	3	5	8	10	13'
'11	9	7	5	2	90-80	2	5	7	9	11'
'10	8	6	4	2	80-70	2	4	6	8	10'
'9	7	5	4	2	70-60	2	4	5	7	9'
'8	6	5	3	2	60-50	2	3	5	6	8'

NOTES ON PERFORMANCE

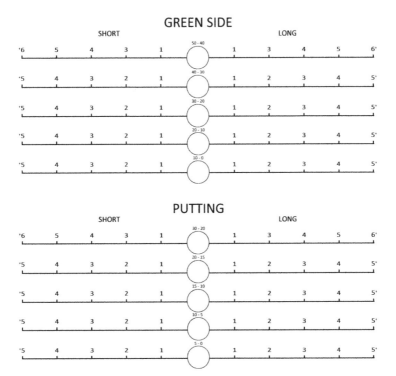

DISPERSION
PERFORMANCE REVIEW

"You don't have to see the whole staircase, just take the first step."
MARTIN LUTHER KING JR

Which 20% of my yardages are resulting in 80% of my **DISPERSION** from the hole?

1) _____

2) _____

3) _____

4) _____

5) _____

What specific drills can I implement, test and work on to improve on the above?

_____

_____

_____

_____

PROXIMITY PERFORMANCE REVIEW

"You can have everything in life you want, if you will just help other people get what they want."
ZIG ZIGLAR

Which 20% of my yardages are resulting in 80% of my **PROXIMITY** from the hole?

1) _____

2) _____

3) _____

4) _____

5) _____

What specific drills can I implement, test and work on to improve on the above?

_____

_____

_____

_____

Course: _____   Score: _____   Date: _____

"There are risks and costs to action. But they are far less than the long range risks of comfortable inaction."

- JOHN F. KENNEDY

LONG GAME

LEFT						RIGHT			
'38	30	23	15	8	300⁺ - 275 ◯ 8	15	23	30	38'
'34	28	21	14	7	275 - 250 ◯ 7	14	21	28	34'
'31	25	19	13	6	250 - 225 ◯ 6	13	19	25	31'
'28	23	17	11	6	225 - 200 ◯ 6	11	17	23	28'
'25	20	15	10	5	200 - 180 ◯ 5	10	15	20	25'

IRON GAME

LEFT						RIGHT			
'15	12	8	6	3	180 - 160 ◯ 3	6	8	12	15'
'14	11	8	6	3	160 - 150 ◯ 3	6	8	11	14'
'13	10	8	5	3	150 - 140 ◯ 3	5	8	10	13'
'11	9	7	5	2	140 - 130 ◯ 2	5	7	9	11'
'10	8	6	4	2	130 - 120 ◯ 2	4	6	8	10'

WEDGE GAME

SHORT						LONG			
'15	12	8	6	3	120 - 110 ◯ 3	6	8	12	15'
'14	11	8	6	3	110 - 100 ◯ 3	6	8	11	14'
'13	10	8	5	3	100 - 90 ◯ 3	5	8	10	13'
'11	9	7	5	2	90 - 80 ◯ 2	5	7	9	11'
'10	8	6	4	2	80 - 70 ◯ 2	4	6	8	10'
'9	7	5	4	2	70 - 60 ◯ 2	4	5	7	9'
'8	6	5	3	2	60 - 50 ◯ 2	3	5	6	8'

NOTES ON PERFORMANCE

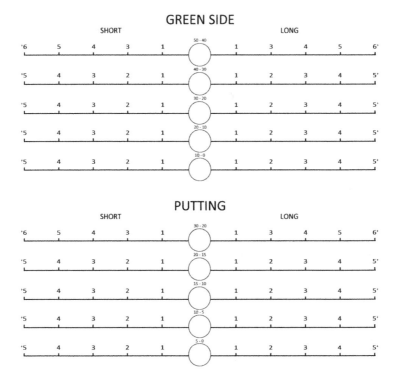

Course: Score: Date:

"Do more than you are being paid to do, and you'll eventually be paid more for what you do."

— ZIG ZIGLAR

LONG GAME

LEFT				300' – 275				RIGHT
'38	30	23	15	8 ○ 8	15	23	30	38'
'34	28	21	14	7 ○ 7 275 – 250	14	21	28	34'
'31	25	19	13	6 ○ 6 250 – 225	13	19	25	31'
'28	23	17	11	6 ○ 6 225 – 200	11	17	23	28'
'25	20	15	10	5 ○ 5 200 – 180	10	15	20	25'

IRON GAME

LEFT				180 – 160				RIGHT
'15	12	8	6	3 ○ 3	6	8	12	15'
'14	11	8	6	3 ○ 3 160 – 150	6	8	11	14'
'13	10	8	5	3 ○ 3 150 – 140	5	8	10	13'
'11	9	7	5	2 ○ 2 140 – 130	5	7	9	11'
'10	8	6	4	2 ○ 2 130 – 120	4	6	8	10'

WEDGE GAME

SHORT				120 – 110				LONG
'15	12	8	6	3 ○ 3	6	8	12	15'
'14	11	8	6	3 ○ 3 110 – 100	6	8	11	14'
'13	10	8	5	3 ○ 3 100 – 90	5	8	10	13'
'11	9	7	5	2 ○ 2 90 – 80	5	7	9	11'
'10	8	6	4	2 ○ 2 80 – 70	4	6	8	10'
'9	7	5	4	2 ○ 2 70 – 60	4	5	7	9'
'8	6	5	3	2 ○ 2 60 – 50	3	5	6	8'

NOTES ON PERFORMANCE

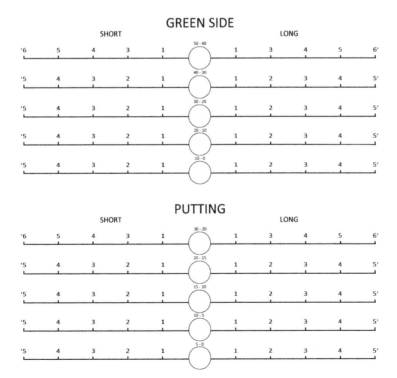

Course: _____   Score: _____   Date: _____

"Do the hard jobs first. The easy jobs will take care of themselves."

- DALE CARNEGIE

LONG GAME

	LEFT						RIGHT		
'38	30	23	15	8	**300+ - 275** ○ 8	15	23	30	38'
'34	28	21	14	7	**275 - 250** ○ 7	14	21	28	34'
'31	25	19	13	6	**250 - 225** ○ 6	13	19	25	31'
'28	23	17	11	6	**225 - 200** ○ 6	11	17	23	28'
'25	20	15	10	5	**200 - 180** ○ 5	10	15	20	25'

IRON GAME

	LEFT						RIGHT		
'15	12	8	6	3	**180 - 160** ○ 3	6	8	12	15'
'14	11	8	6	3	**160 - 150** ○ 3	6	8	11	14'
'13	10	8	5	3	**150 - 140** ○ 3	5	8	10	13'
'11	9	7	5	2	**140 - 130** ○ 2	5	7	9	11'
'10	8	6	4	2	**130 - 120** ○ 2	4	6	8	10'

WEDGE GAME

	SHORT						LONG		
'15	12	8	6	3	**120 - 110** ○ 3	6	8	12	15'
'14	11	8	6	3	**110 - 100** ○ 3	6	8	11	14'
'13	10	8	5	3	**100 - 90** ○ 3	5	8	10	13'
'11	9	7	5	2	**90 - 80** ○ 2	5	7	9	11'
'10	8	6	4	2	**80 - 70** ○ 2	4	6	8	10'
'9	7	5	4	2	**70 - 60** ○ 2	4	5	7	9'
'8	6	5	3	2	**60 - 50** ○ 2	3	5	6	8'

NOTES ON PERFORMANCE

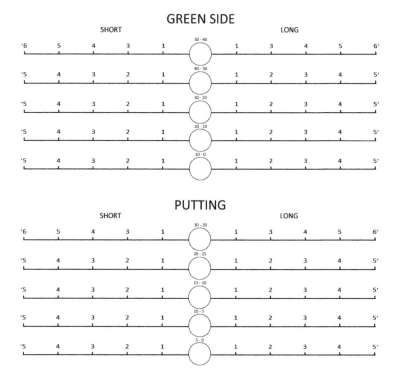

Course: _____ Score: _____ Date: _____

"Real integrity is doing the right thing, knowing that nobody's going to know whether you did it or not."

— OPRAH WINFREY

LONG GAME

LEFT					300' - 275					RIGHT
'38	30	23	15	8	○	8	15	23	30	38'
'34	28	21	14	7	275 - 250 ○	7	14	21	28	34'
'31	25	19	13	6	250 - 225 ○	6	13	19	25	31'
'28	23	17	11	6	225 - 200 ○	6	11	17	23	28'
'25	20	15	10	5	200 - 180 ○	5	10	15	20	25'

IRON GAME

LEFT					180 - 160					RIGHT
'15	12	8	6	3	○	3	6	8	12	15'
'14	11	8	6	3	160 - 150 ○	3	6	8	11	14'
'13	10	8	5	3	150 - 140 ○	3	5	8	10	13'
'11	9	7	5	2	140 - 130 ○	2	5	7	9	11'
'10	8	6	4	2	130 - 120 ○	2	4	6	8	10'

WEDGE GAME

SHORT					120 - 110					LONG
'15	12	8	6	3	○	3	6	8	12	15'
'14	11	8	6	3	110 - 100 ○	3	6	8	11	14'
'13	10	8	5	3	100 - 90 ○	3	5	8	10	13'
'11	9	7	5	2	90 - 80 ○	2	5	7	9	11'
'10	8	6	4	2	80 - 70 ○	2	4	6	8	10'
'9	7	5	4	2	70 - 60 ○	2	4	5	7	9'
'8	6	5	3	2	60 - 50 ○	2	3	5	6	8'

NOTES ON PERFORMANCE

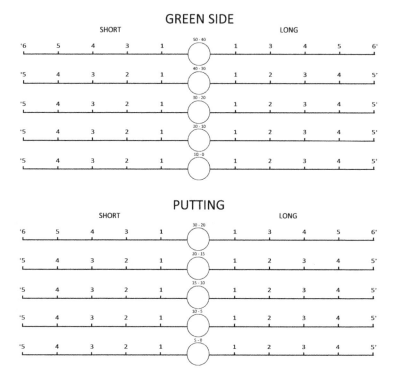

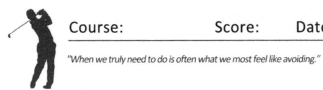

Course: _____ Score: _____ Date: _____

"When we truly need to do is often what we most feel like avoiding."

— DAVID ALLEN

LONG GAME

LEFT						RIGHT			
'38	30	23	15	8	300'–275	8	15	23	30	38'
'34	28	21	14	7	275–250	7	14	21	28	34'
'31	25	19	13	6	250–225	6	13	19	25	31'
'28	23	17	11	6	225–200	6	11	17	23	28'
'25	20	15	10	5	200–180	5	10	15	20	25'

IRON GAME

LEFT						RIGHT			
'15	12	8	6	3	180–160	3	6	8	12	15'
'14	11	8	6	3	160–150	3	6	8	11	14'
'13	10	8	5	3	150–140	3	5	8	10	13'
'11	9	7	5	2	140–130	2	5	7	9	11'
'10	8	6	4	2	130–120	2	4	6	8	10'

WEDGE GAME

SHORT						LONG			
'15	12	8	6	3	120–110	3	6	8	12	15'
'14	11	8	6	3	110–100	3	6	8	11	14'
'13	10	8	5	3	100–90	3	5	8	10	13'
'11	9	7	5	2	90–80	2	5	7	9	11'
'10	8	6	4	2	80–70	2	4	6	8	10'
'9	7	5	4	2	70–60	2	4	5	7	9'
'8	6	5	3	2	60–50	2	3	5	6	8'

NOTES ON PERFORMANCE

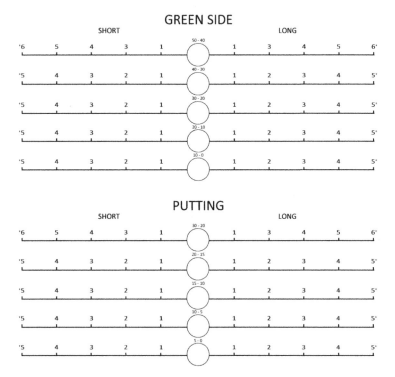

Course: _____ Score: _____ Date: _____

"While one person hesitates because he feels inferior, the other is busy making mistakes and becoming superior."

— HENRY LINK

LONG GAME

LEFT								RIGHT	
'38	30	23	15	8	300'–275 ○ 8	15	23	30	38'
'34	28	21	14	7	275–250 ○ 7	14	21	28	34'
'31	25	19	13	6	250–225 ○ 6	13	19	25	31'
'28	23	17	11	6	225–200 ○ 6	11	17	23	28'
'25	20	15	10	5	200–180 ○ 5	10	15	20	25'

IRON GAME

LEFT								RIGHT	
'15	12	8	6	3	180–160 ○ 3	6	8	12	15'
'14	11	8	6	3	160–150 ○ 3	6	8	11	14'
'13	10	8	5	3	150–140 ○ 3	5	8	10	13'
'11	9	7	5	2	140–130 ○ 2	5	7	9	11'
'10	8	6	4	2	130–120 ○ 2	4	6	8	10'

WEDGE GAME

SHORT								LONG	
'15	12	8	6	3	120–110 ○ 3	6	8	12	15'
'14	11	8	6	3	110–100 ○ 3	6	8	11	14'
'13	10	8	5	3	100–90 ○ 3	5	8	10	13'
'11	9	7	5	2	90–80 ○ 2	5	7	9	11'
'10	8	6	4	2	80–70 ○ 2	4	6	8	10'
'9	7	5	4	2	70–60 ○ 2	4	5	7	9'
'8	6	5	3	2	60–50 ○ 2	3	5	6	8'

NOTES ON PERFORMANCE

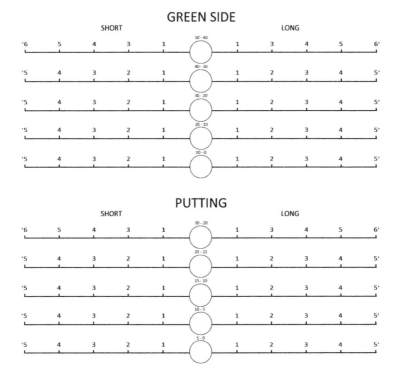

DISPERSION
PERFORMANCE REVIEW

"Until we can manage time, we can manage nothing else."
PETER F. DRUCKER

Which 20% of my yardages are resulting in 80% of my **DISPERSION** from the hole?

1) _____

2) _____

3) _____

4) _____

5) _____

What specific drills can I implement, test and work on to improve on the above?

_____

_____

_____

_____

PROXIMITY PERFORMANCE REVIEW

"Simplicity boils down to two steps: Identify the essential. Eliminate the rest."
LEO BABAUTA

Which 20% of my yardages are resulting in 80% of my **PROXIMITY** from the hole?

1) _____

2) _____

3) _____

4) _____

5) _____

What specific drills can I implement, test and work on to improve on the above?

_____

_____

_____

_____

Course: Score: Date:

"Go confidently in the direction of your dreams! Live the life you've imagined."

- HENRY DAVID THOREAU

LONG GAME

LEFT								RIGHT			
'38	30	23	15	8	300'-275	8	15	23	30	38'
'34	28	21	14	7	275-250	7	14	21	28	34'
'31	25	19	13	6	250-225	6	13	19	25	31'
'28	23	17	11	6	225-200	6	11	17	23	28'
'25	20	15	10	5	200-180	5	10	15	20	25'

IRON GAME

LEFT								RIGHT			
'15	12	8	6	3	180-160	3	6	8	12	15'
'14	11	8	6	3	160-150	3	6	8	11	14'
'13	10	8	5	3	150-140	3	5	8	10	13'
'11	9	7	5	2	140-130	2	5	7	9	11'
'10	8	6	4	2	130-120	2	4	6	8	10'

WEDGE GAME

SHORT								LONG			
'15	12	8	6	3	120-110	3	6	8	12	15'
'14	11	8	6	3	110-100	3	6	8	11	14'
'13	10	8	5	3	100-90	3	5	8	10	13'
'11	9	7	5	2	90-80	2	5	7	9	11'
'10	8	6	4	2	80-70	2	4	6	8	10'
'9	7	5	4	2	70-60	2	4	5	7	9'
'8	6	5	3	2	60-50	2	3	5	6	8'

NOTES ON PERFORMANCE

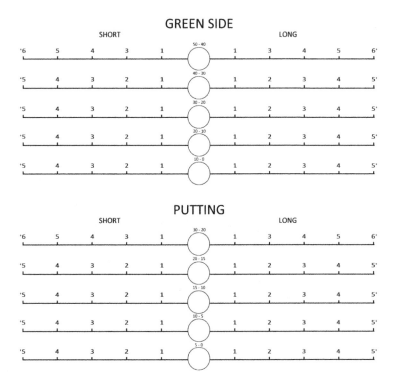

Course: _____ Score: _____ Date: _____

"Good friends, good books, and a sleepy conscience: this is the ideal life."

- MARK TWAIN

LONG GAME

LEFT							RIGHT			
					300' - 275					
'38	30	23	15	8	○	8	15	23	30	38'
					275 - 250					
'34	28	21	14	7	○	7	14	21	28	34'
					250 - 225					
'31	25	19	13	6	○	6	13	19	25	31'
					225 - 200					
'28	23	17	11	6	○	6	11	17	23	28'
					200 - 180					
'25	20	15	10	5	○	5	10	15	20	25'

IRON GAME

LEFT							RIGHT			
					180 - 160					
'15	12	8	6	3	○	3	6	8	12	15'
					160 - 150					
'14	11	8	6	3	○	3	6	8	11	14'
					150 - 140					
'13	10	8	5	3	○	3	5	8	10	13'
					140 - 130					
'11	9	7	5	2	○	2	5	7	9	11'
					130 - 120					
'10	8	6	4	2	○	2	4	6	8	10'

WEDGE GAME

SHORT							LONG			
					120 - 110					
'15	12	8	6	3	○	3	6	8	12	15'
					110 - 100					
'14	11	8	6	3	○	3	6	8	11	14'
					100 - 90					
'13	10	8	5	3	○	3	5	8	10	13'
					90 - 80					
'11	9	7	5	2	○	2	5	7	9	11'
					80 - 70					
'10	8	6	4	2	○	2	4	6	8	10'
					70 - 60					
'9	7	5	4	2	○	2	4	5	7	9'
					60 - 50					
'8	6	5	3	2	○	2	3	5	6	8'

NOTES ON PERFORMANCE

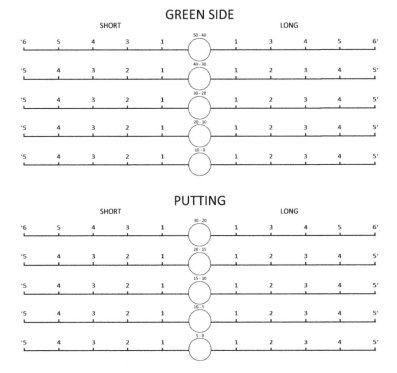

Course: _____ **Score:** _____ **Date:** _____

"Work Hard, have fun, make history"

— JEFF BEZOS

LONG GAME

	LEFT							RIGHT	
'38	30	23	15	8	300'–275	8	15	23	30	38'
'34	28	21	14	7	275–250	7	14	21	28	34'
'31	25	19	13	6	250–225	6	13	19	25	31'
'28	23	17	11	6	225–200	6	11	17	23	28'
'25	20	15	10	5	200–180	5	10	15	20	25'

IRON GAME

	LEFT							RIGHT	
'15	12	8	6	3	180–160	3	6	8	12	15'
'14	11	8	6	3	160–150	3	6	8	11	14'
'13	10	8	5	3	150–140	3	5	8	10	13'
'11	9	7	5	2	140–130	2	5	7	9	11'
'10	8	6	4	2	130–120	2	4	6	8	10'

WEDGE GAME

	SHORT							LONG	
'15	12	8	6	3	120–110	3	6	8	12	15'
'14	11	8	6	3	110–100	3	6	8	11	14'
'13	10	8	5	3	100–90	3	5	8	10	13'
'11	9	7	5	2	90–80	2	5	7	9	11'
'10	8	6	4	2	80–70	2	4	6	8	10'
'9	7	5	4	2	70–60	2	4	5	7	9'
'8	6	5	3	2	60–50	2	3	5	6	8'

NOTES ON PERFORMANCE

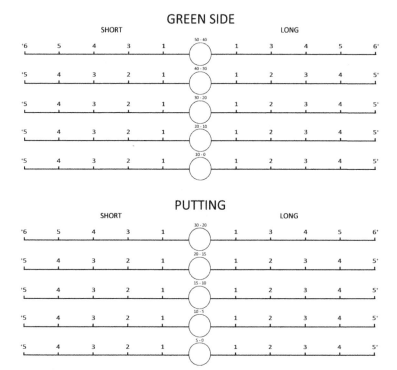

Course: Score: Date:

"Nothing will work unless you do."

— MAYA ANGELOU

LONG GAME

LEFT						RIGHT			
'38	30	23	15	8	**300' – 275**	8	15	23	30	38'
'34	28	21	14	7	**275 – 250**	7	14	21	28	34'
'31	25	19	13	6	**250 – 225**	6	13	19	25	31'
'28	23	17	11	6	**225 – 200**	6	11	17	23	28'
'25	20	15	10	5	**200 – 180**	5	10	15	20	25'

IRON GAME

LEFT						RIGHT			
'15	12	8	6	3	**180 – 160**	3	6	8	12	15'
'14	11	8	6	3	**160 – 150**	3	6	8	11	14'
'13	10	8	5	3	**150 – 140**	3	5	8	10	13'
'11	9	7	5	2	**140 – 130**	2	5	7	9	11'
'10	8	6	4	2	**130 – 120**	2	4	6	8	10'

WEDGE GAME

SHORT						LONG			
'15	12	8	6	3	**120 – 110**	3	6	8	12	15'
'14	11	8	6	3	**110 – 100**	3	6	8	11	14'
'13	10	8	5	3	**100 – 90**	3	5	8	10	13'
'11	9	7	5	2	**90 – 80**	2	5	7	9	11'
'10	8	6	4	2	**80 – 70**	2	4	6	8	10'
'9	7	5	4	2	**70 – 60**	2	4	5	7	9'
'8	6	5	3	2	**60 – 50**	2	3	5	6	8'

NOTES ON PERFORMANCE

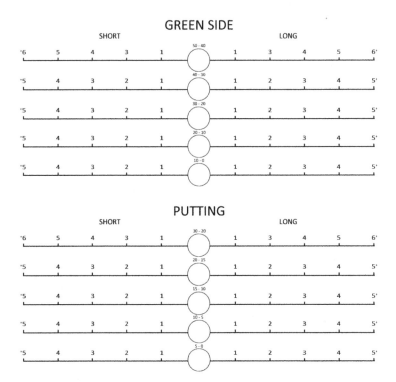

Course: _____ Score: _____ Date: _____

"A mind that is stretched by a new experience can never go back to its old dimensions."

- OLIVER WENDELL HOLMES, JR.

LONG GAME

LEFT						RIGHT			
'38	30	23	15	8	300+ - 275	8	15	23	30	38'
'34	28	21	14	7	275 - 250	7	14	21	28	34'
'31	25	19	13	6	250 - 225	6	13	19	25	31'
'28	23	17	11	6	225 - 200	6	11	17	23	28'
'25	20	15	10	5	200 - 180	5	10	15	20	25'

IRON GAME

LEFT						RIGHT			
'15	12	8	6	3	180 - 160	3	6	8	12	15'
'14	11	8	6	3	160 - 150	3	6	8	11	14'
'13	10	8	5	3	150 - 140	3	5	8	10	13'
'11	9	7	5	2	140 - 130	2	5	7	9	11'
'10	8	6	4	2	130 - 120	2	4	6	8	10'

WEDGE GAME

SHORT						LONG			
'15	12	8	6	3	120 - 110	3	6	8	12	15'
'14	11	8	6	3	110 - 100	3	6	8	11	14'
'13	10	8	5	3	100 - 90	3	5	8	10	13'
'11	9	7	5	2	90 - 80	2	5	7	9	11'
'10	8	6	4	2	80 - 70	2	4	6	8	10'
'9	7	5	4	2	70 - 60	2	4	5	7	9'
'8	6	5	3	2	60 - 50	2	3	5	6	8'

NOTES ON PERFORMANCE

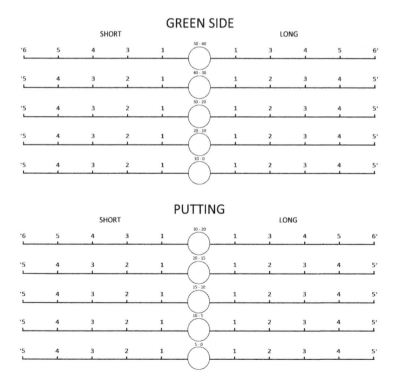

Course: _____ Score: _____ Date: _____

"If you don't like something change it; if you can't change it, change the way you think about it."

- MARY ENGELBREIT

LONG GAME

		LEFT					RIGHT			
'38	30	23	15	8	300+ - 275	8	15	23	30	38'
'34	28	21	14	7	275 - 250	7	14	21	28	34'
'31	25	19	13	6	250 - 225	6	13	19	25	31'
'28	23	17	11	6	225 - 200	6	11	17	23	28'
'25	20	15	10	5	200 - 180	5	10	15	20	25'

IRON GAME

		LEFT					RIGHT			
'15	12	8	6	3	180 - 160	3	6	8	12	15'
'14	11	8	6	3	160 - 150	3	6	8	11	14'
'13	10	8	5	3	150 - 140	3	5	8	10	13'
'11	9	7	5	2	140 - 130	2	5	7	9	11'
'10	8	6	4	2	130 - 120	2	4	6	8	10'

WEDGE GAME

		SHORT					LONG			
'15	12	8	6	3	120 - 110	3	6	8	12	15'
'14	11	8	6	3	110 - 100	3	6	8	11	14'
'13	10	8	5	3	100 - 90	3	5	8	10	13'
'11	9	7	5	2	90 - 80	2	5	7	9	11'
'10	8	6	4	2	80 - 70	2	4	6	8	10'
'9	7	5	4	2	70 - 60	2	4	5	7	9'
'8	6	5	3	2	60 - 50	2	3	5	6	8'

NOTES ON PERFORMANCE

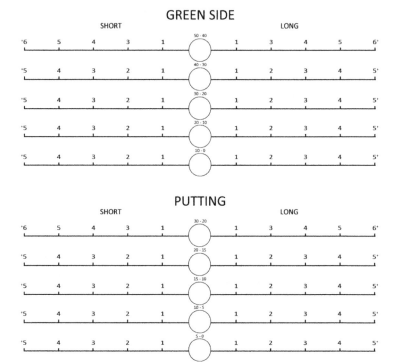

DISPERSION
PERFORMANCE REVIEW

"Be willing to go all out, in pursuit of your dream. Ultimately it will pay off. You are more powerful than you think you are."
LES BROWN

Which 20% of my yardages are resulting in 80% of my DISPERSION from the hole?

1) _____
2) _____
3) _____
4) _____
5) _____

What specific drills can I implement, test and work on to improve on the above?

_____
_____
_____
_____

PROXIMITY PERFORMANCE REVIEW

"If You Are Working On Something That You Really Care About, You Don't Have To Be Pushed. The Vision Pulls You."
STEVE JOBS

Which 20% of my yardages are resulting in 80% of my **PROXIMITY** from the hole?

1) _____

2) _____

3) _____

4) _____

5) _____

What specific drills can I implement, test and work on to improve on the above?

_____

_____

_____

_____

SCORE BETTER

Track your stats against the worlds best.

LONG GAME
300 - 250 YARDS

Rank	Player	Yards	Your Data
1	Ryan Palmer	16	
2	Patrick Cantlay	16.1	
3	Sung Kang	16.3	
4	Keegan Bradley	16.9	
5	Xander Schauffele	17.3	
6	Michael Thompson	17.7	
T7	Kiradech Aphibarnrat	18	
T7	Chad Campbell	18	
T7	Bryson DeChambeau	18	
T7	Si Woo Kim	18	

250 - 225

Rank	Player	Yards	Your Data
1	Louis Oosthuizen	13.3	
2	Matt Every	13.9	
3	Bryson DeChambeau	14.1	
4	Francesco Molinari	14.4	
5	Justin Thomas	14.5	
6	Lanto Griffin	14.6	
7	Byeong Hun An	14.7	
8	Jonathan Byrd	14.8	
9	Webb Simpson	14.9	
10	Troy Merritt	44' 6"	

225 - 200

Rank	Player	Yards	Your Data
1	Bronson Burgoon	11.2	
2	Paul Casey	11.4	
3	Brooks Koepka	11.5	
4	Henrik Stenson	11.6	
5	Branden Grace	11.7	
6	Jason Kokrak	11.8	
7	Nate Lashley	11.9	
T8	Keith Mitchell	12	
T8	Jon Rahm	12	
T10	Justin Thomas	12.1	

(Data collected from PGA Tour)

200 - 180

Rank	Player	Yards	Your Data
1	Tom Hoge	9.4	
2	Tiger Woods	9.5	
3	Hideki Matsuyama	9.6	
T4	Sung Kang	9.7	
T4	Shane Lowry	9.7	
6	Nick Watney	9.8	
7	Gary Woodland	9.7	
8	Francesco Molinari	10	
9	Chez Reavie	10.1	
T10	Rickie Fowler	10.2	

IRON GAME
180 - 150 YARDS

Rank	Player	Yards	Your Data
1	Kevin Na	8	
2	Cameron Percy	8.1	
T3	Brooks Koepka	8.2	
T3	Marc Leishman	8.2	
T3	Henrik Stenson	8.2	
T6	Zecheng Dou	8.4	
T6	Cody Gribble	8.4	
T6	Zach Johnson	8.4	
9	Patton Kizzire	9	
10	Phil Mickelson	9.1	

150 - 125

Rank	Player	Yards	Your Data
1	Jordan Spieth	6.3	
T2	Wesley Bryan	6.5	
T2	Rory McIlroy	6.5	
T4	Zach Johnson	6.6	
T4	Chris Kirk	6.6	
6	Nick Watney	6.8	
7	Satoshi Kodaira	6.9	
8	Blayne Barber	7.1	
T9	Whee Kim	7.2	
T9	Tiger Woods	7.2	

WEDGE GAME
120 - 100 YARDS

Rank	Player	Yards	Your Data
1	Wesley Bryan	5.2	
2	Zac Blair	5.4	
3	Kevin Na	5.5	
4	Kyle Thompson	5.6	
5	Ryan Armour	5.7	
T6	Alex Cejka	5.9	
T6	Sam Ryder	5.9	
8	John Huh	6	
T9	Fabián Gómez	6.1	
10	Robert Streb	6.2	

100 - 75

Rank	Player	Yards	Your Data
1	Robert Streb	3.4	
T2	Stewart Cink	4.5	
T2	Justin Thomas	4.5	
4	Tiger Woods	4.6	
T5	Brian Gay	4.7	
T5	Ben Martin	4.7	
T7	Chad Campbell	4.8	
T7	Rory McIlroy	4.8	
9	Ryan Blaum	4.9	
10	Danny Lee	5	

75 - 50

Rank	Player	Yards	Your Data
1	Vaughn Taylor	2.4	
2	Pat Perez	2.7	
3	Tiger Woods	3.1	
4	Jon Rahm	3.2	
5	Wesley Bryan	3.3	
6	Mackenzie Hughes	3.4	
7	Dustin Johnson	3.4	
T8	Lucas Glover	3.5	
T8	Alex Noren	3.6	
T10	Jonathan Byrd	3.7	

GREENSIDE
50 - 30 YARDS

Rank	Player	Yards	Your Data
1	Jim Furyk	2.7	
2	Wesley Bryan	2.8	
3	Branden Grace	3.2	
4	Danny Lee	3.3	
5	Louis Oosthuizen	3.4	
6	Patrick Reed	3.5	
T7	Austin Cook	3.6	
T7	Ryan Moore	3.6	
T9	Jonathan Byrd	3.7	
T9	Webb Simpson	3.7	

30 - 20

Rank	Player	Yards	Your Data
1	Alex Cejka	2.5	
T2	Tyrrell Hatton	2.6	
T2	Louis Oosthuizen	2.6	
4	Rob Oppenheim	2.6	
T5	Daniel Summerhays	2.6	
T5	Wesley Bryan	2.7	
T7	Danny Lee	2.7	
T7	C.T. Pan	2.7	
9	Aaron Baddeley	2.9	
10	Nate Lashley	2.9	

20 - 10

Rank	Player	Yards	Your Data
1	Martin Laird	1.9	
2	Justin Thomas	2	
3	Tiger Woods	2	
4	Bud Cauley	2.2	
5	Cameron Percy	2.2	
6	Ricky Barnes	2.3	
7	Jamie Lovemark	2.3	
T8	Jonathan Byrd	2.4	
T8	Ryan Moore	2.4	
T10	Kevin Na	2.4	

< 10

Rank	Player	Yards	Your Data
1	Johnson Wagner	0.8	
2	D.A. Points	0.9	
T3	Kiradech Aphibarnrat	1	
T3	Jim Furyk	1	
T5	Ben Crane	1.1	
T5	Peter Malnati	1.1	
T7	Bud Cauley	1.2	
T7	Zach Johnson	1.2	
T7	Russell Knox	1.2	
T10	Dominic Bozzelli	1.3	

LONG GAME IRON GAME
DRILLS

[300 - 120 YARDS]

- Make your range time more effective.
- Implement pressure to your range sessions.
- Eliminate your big miss.

The following drills have been taken from research at Making A Club Champion: Long Game Golf Journal: Your Guide To Effective Practice Habits And High Performance Routines

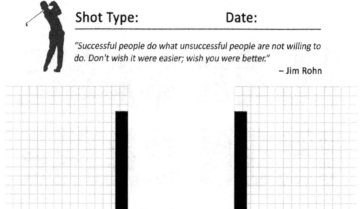

Shot Type: _____ Date: _____

"Successful people do what unsuccessful people are not willing to do. Don't wish it were easier; wish you were better."

– Jim Rohn

Long Game and Iron Game Drills

Goal

To score the most points in 10 shots.

Drill

- Pick out your intended yardage for your days practice.

- Take out 10 balls on the range.

- Pick two targets to hit the ball through. You can start off wide and narrow your targets with time.

- Mark an (x) where your ball lands and use the boxes above to track your scores.

Shot Type: 150 Yards   **Date:** Sep 12, 2017

EXAMPLE PAGE

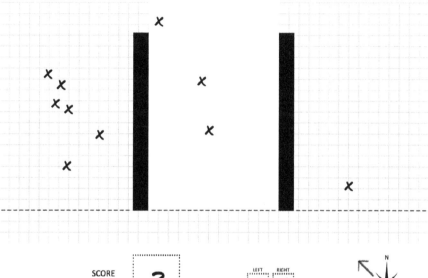

SCORE TARGET ZONE: 3   **MISSES** LEFT: 6 RIGHT: 1   **WIND:** NW

Notes

- 8 iron, wind ← right.
- Aim small, miss small. Identify precise targets.
- Go through routine on each shot. Each shot counts!
- Feel like you are coming more from the inside.
- Take the wind into account next time.

Shot Type: _____   **Date:** _____

"The successful warrior is the average man, with laser-like focus."

– Bruce Lee

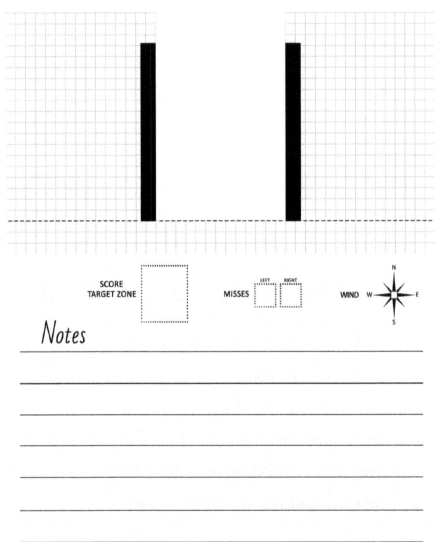

SCORE TARGET ZONE ▢   MISSES LEFT ▢ RIGHT ▢   WIND N/W/E/S

Notes

_____
_____
_____
_____
_____
_____
_____

Shot Type: _____   Date: _____

"Twenty years from now, you will be more disappointed by the things that you didn't do than by the ones you did do."

– Mark Twain

SCORE TARGET ZONE   MISSES LEFT RIGHT   WIND N W E S

Notes

_____

_____

_____

_____

_____

_____

_____

Shot Type: _____   Date: _____

"Only put off until tomorrow what you are willing to die having left undone."

– Pablo Picasso

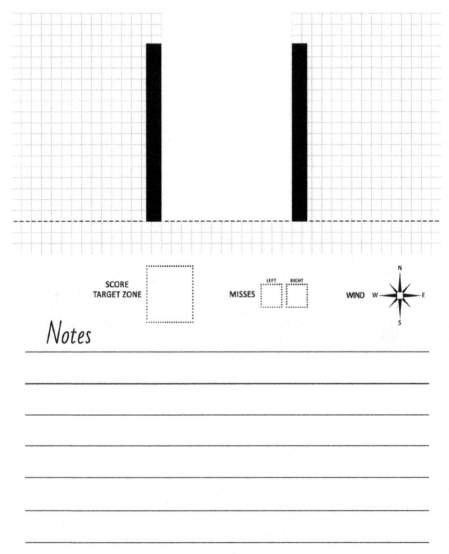

SCORE TARGET ZONE □   MISSES LEFT □ RIGHT □   WIND N/S/E/W

Notes

_____
_____
_____
_____
_____
_____
_____

Shot Type: _____   Date: _____

"Success is the sum of small efforts, repeated day in and day out."

– Robert Collier

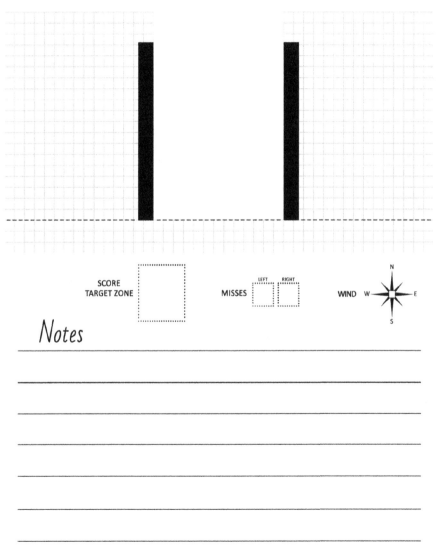

SCORE TARGET ZONE   MISSES LEFT RIGHT   WIND N W E S

Notes

_____
_____
_____
_____
_____
_____
_____

Shot Type: _____   **Date:** _____

"If you can't explain it simply, you don't understand it well enough."

– Albert Einstein

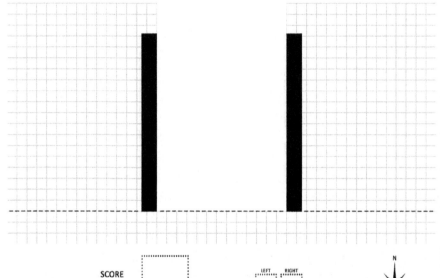

SCORE TARGET ZONE | MISSES LEFT RIGHT | WIND N W E S

Notes

_____
_____
_____
_____
_____
_____
_____

Shot Type: _____ **Date:** _____

"Don't be afraid to give up the good to go for the great."

– John D. Rockefeller

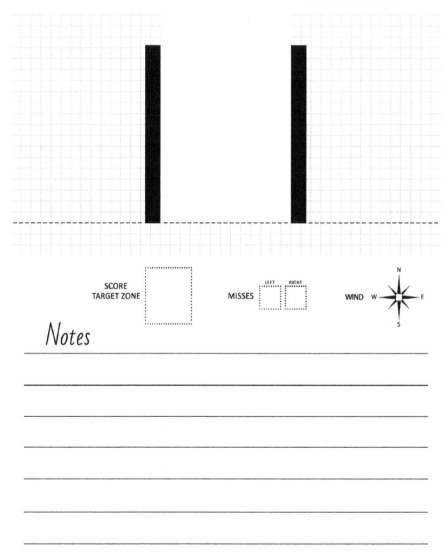

SCORE TARGET ZONE

MISSES LEFT RIGHT

WIND N W E S

Notes

_____
_____
_____
_____
_____
_____
_____

Shot Type: _____   Date: _____

"No one can make you feel inferior without your consent."

– Eleanor Roosevelt

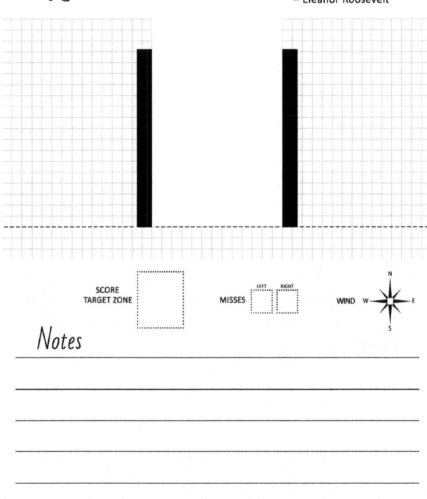

SCORE TARGET ZONE

MISSES LEFT RIGHT

WIND

Notes

_____
_____
_____
_____
_____
_____
_____

Shot Type: _____ Date: _____

"Whenever you see a successful person, you only see the public glories, never the private sacrifices to reach them."

— Vaibhav Shah

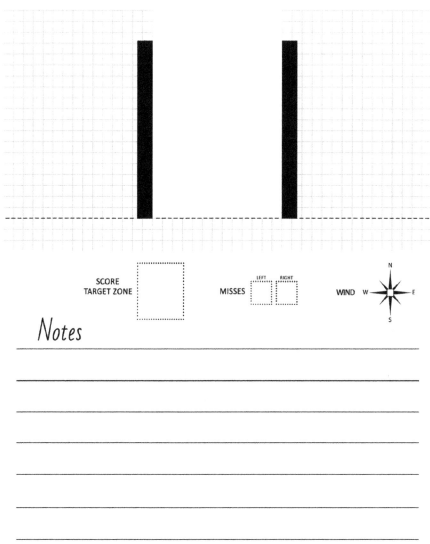

SCORE TARGET ZONE MISSES (LEFT / RIGHT) WIND

Notes

_____

_____

_____

_____

_____

_____

_____

Shot Type: _____   Date: _____

"If you are not willing to risk the usual, you will have to settle for the ordinary."

– Winston Churchill

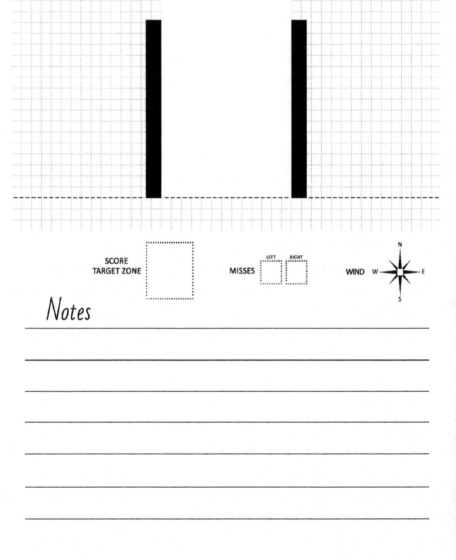

SCORE TARGET ZONE   MISSES LEFT RIGHT   WIND

Notes

_____
_____
_____
_____
_____
_____
_____

Shot Type: _____   Date: _____

"If you are not willing to risk the usual, you will have to settle for the ordinary."

– Jim Rohn

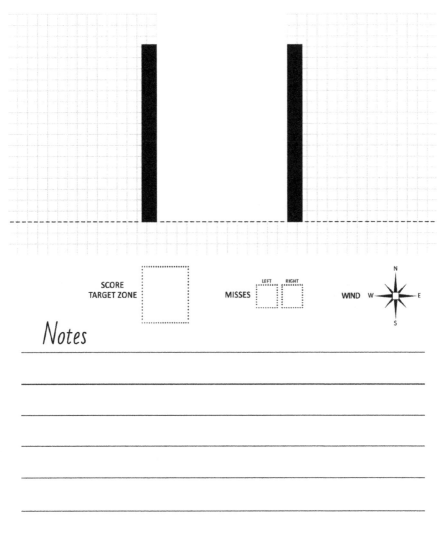

SCORE TARGET ZONE   MISSES LEFT RIGHT   WIND N W E S

Notes

_____
_____
_____
_____
_____
_____
_____

Shot Type: _____ **Date:** _____

"Eliminate one side of the golf course, is a hallmark of great players from Hogan and Locke to Nicklaus and Trevino."

– Hank Haney

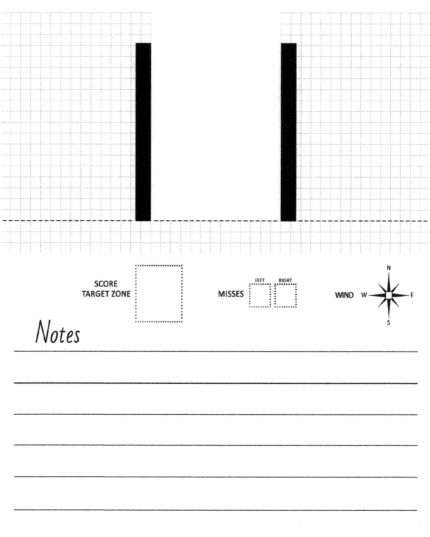

SCORE TARGET ZONE

MISSES LEFT RIGHT

WIND N W E S

Notes

_____

_____

_____

_____

_____

_____

Shot Type: _____ Date: _____

"Success usually comes to those who are too busy to be looking for it."

– Henry David Thoreau

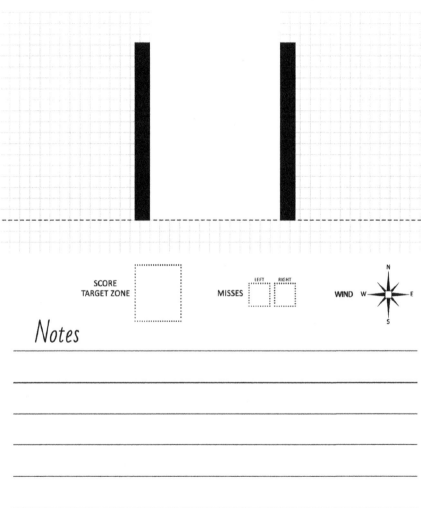

SCORE TARGET ZONE MISSES LEFT RIGHT WIND N W E S

Notes

_____
_____
_____
_____
_____
_____
_____

Shot Type: _____   **Date:** _____

"Many of life's failures are people who did not realize how close they were to success when they gave up."

— Thomas A. Edison

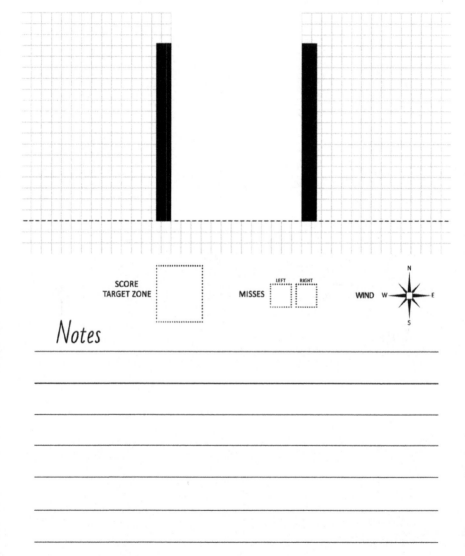

SCORE TARGET ZONE

MISSES   LEFT   RIGHT

WIND   N W — E S

Notes

_____
_____
_____
_____
_____
_____

Shot Type: _____   Date: _____

"You may have to fight a battle more than once to win it."

– Margaret Thatcher

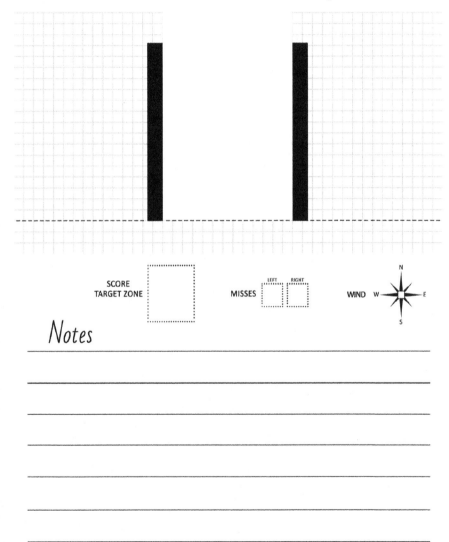

SCORE TARGET ZONE   MISSES LEFT RIGHT   WIND N W E S

Notes

_____
_____
_____
_____
_____
_____
_____
_____

Shot Type: _____   Date: _____

"Courage is resistance to fear, mastery of fear -- not the absence of fear."

– Mark Twain

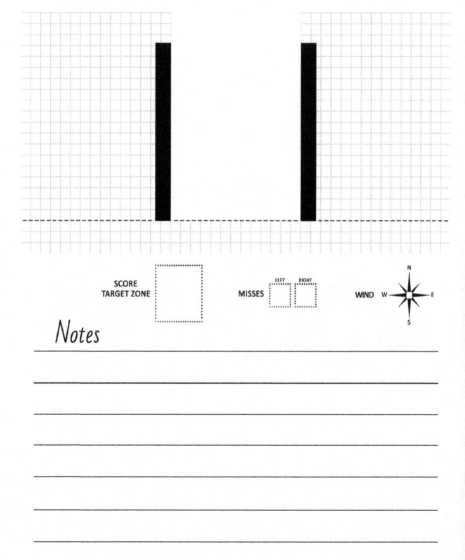

SCORE TARGET ZONE   MISSES LEFT RIGHT   WIND N W E S

Notes

_____
_____
_____
_____
_____
_____
_____

WEDGE GAME GREEN SIDE
DRILLS

[120 - 10 YARDS]

- Improve your distance control.
- Identify your most common misses.
- Analyze your short game practice sessions.

The following drills have been taken from research at Making A Club Champion: Short Game Golf Journal: Your Guide To Effective Practice Habits And High Performance Routines

Shot Type: **70 Yards**   Date: **Sep 12, 2017**

HOW TO PAGE

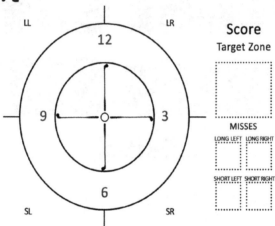

Wedge Game and Green Side Drills

Goal

To score the most points in 10 shots.

Drill

- Take out your driver and place the grip at the hole and mark out four tee pegs at 12' oclock, 3 oclock, 6 oclock and 9 oclock This marks out the "Target Zone."

- Pace out or bushnell your intended yardage for your days practice, which you have been struggling at.

- Take out 10 balls and a specific yardage from your journal One point per ball in the target zone.

- Mark an (x) where your ball lands and use the boxes above to track your scores.

Shot Type: 70 Yards   Date: Sep 12, 2017

EXAMPLE PAGE

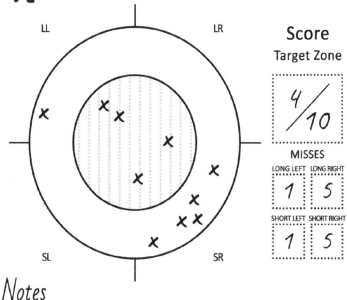

Score
Target Zone

4/10

MISSES

LONG LEFT LONG RIGHT
1   5

SHORT LEFT SHORT RIGHT
1   5

Notes

- Sand Wedge 10 o'clock swing.
- Wind off the right.
- Execute your routine on each shot.
- Process takes care of the results.
- Soft grip pressure.

Shot Type: _____ Date: _____

"The fight is won or lost far away from witnesses – behind the lines, in the gym, and out there on the road, long before I dance under those lights."
— Muhammad Ali

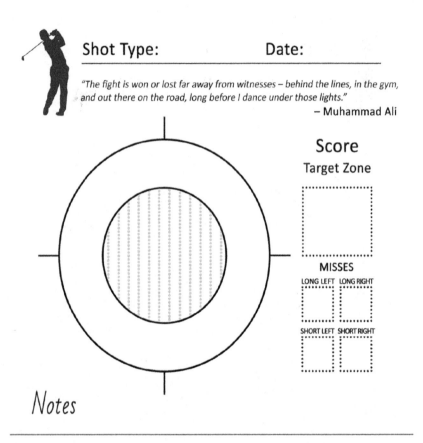

Score
Target Zone

MISSES
LONG LEFT LONG RIGHT

SHORT LEFT SHORT RIGHT

Notes

_____
_____
_____
_____
_____
_____
_____
_____

Shot Type: _____ Date: _____

"The difference between the impossible and the possible lies in a person's determination."

– Tommy Lasorda

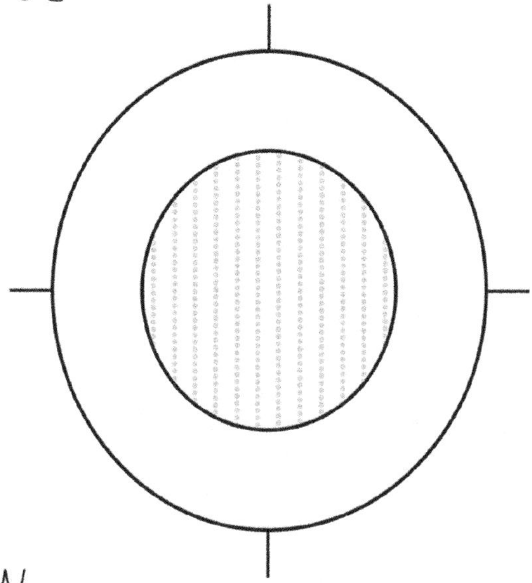

Score
Target Zone

MISSES
LONG LEFT   LONG RIGHT

SHORT LEFT   SHORT RIGHT

Notes

Shot Type: _____   Date: _____

"You're never a loser until you quit trying."

– Mike Ditka

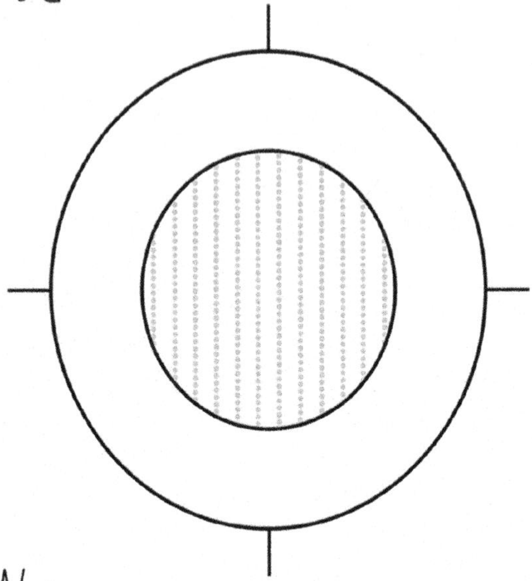

Score
Target Zone

MISSES

LONG LEFT   LONG RIGHT

SHORT LEFT   SHORT RIGHT

Notes

_____
_____
_____
_____
_____
_____
_____
_____
_____

Shot Type: _____ Date: _____

"It's not whether you get knocked down; it's whether you get up."
— Vince Lombardi

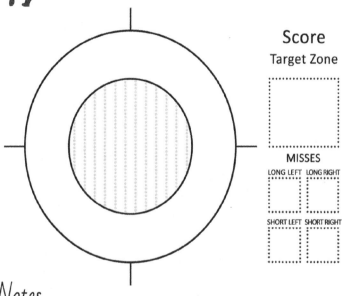

Score
Target Zone

MISSES
LONG LEFT   LONG RIGHT

SHORT LEFT   SHORT RIGHT

Notes

_____
_____
_____
_____
_____
_____
_____
_____
_____

Shot Type: **Date:**

"Gold medals aren't really made of gold. They're made of sweat, determination, and a hard-to-find alloy called guts."

– Dan Gable

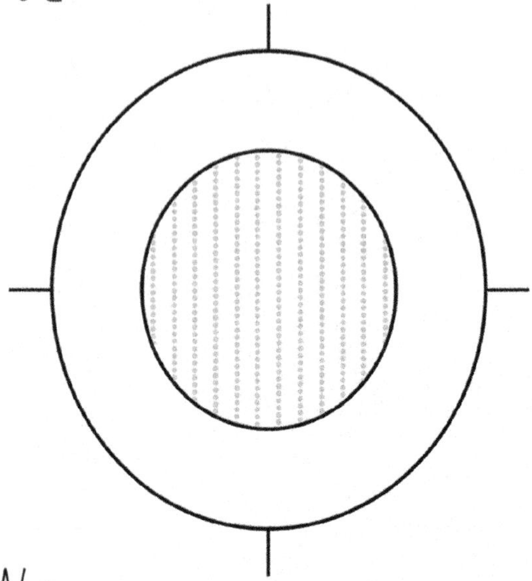

Score
Target Zone

MISSES
LONG LEFT   LONG RIGHT

SHORT LEFT   SHORT RIGHT

Notes

Shot Type: _____ Date: _____

"You miss 100 percent of the shots you don't take."
— Wayne Gretzky

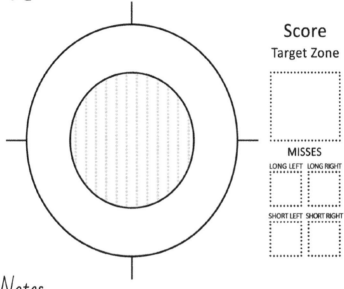

Score
Target Zone

MISSES
LONG LEFT   LONG RIGHT

SHORT LEFT SHORT RIGHT

Notes

_____
_____
_____
_____
_____
_____
_____
_____

Shot Type: _____   **Date:** _____

"Never give up! Failure and rejection are only the first step to succeeding."

– Jim Valvano

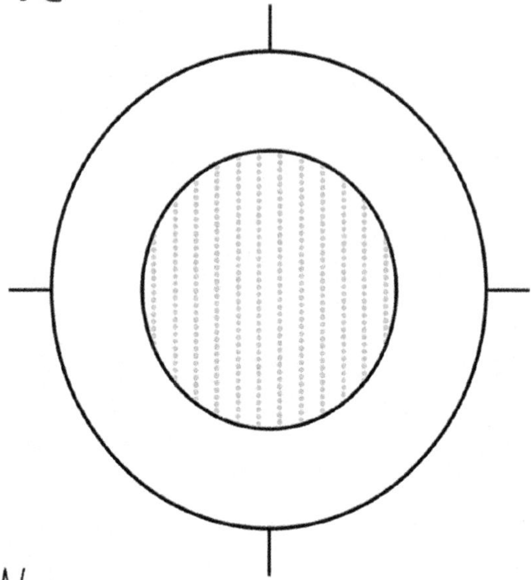

Score
Target Zone

MISSES
LONG LEFT   LONG RIGHT

SHORT LEFT   SHORT RIGHT

Notes

Shot Type: _____   Date: _____

"I hated every minute of training, but I said, 'Don't quit. Suffer now and live the rest of your life as a champion."

— Muhammad Ali

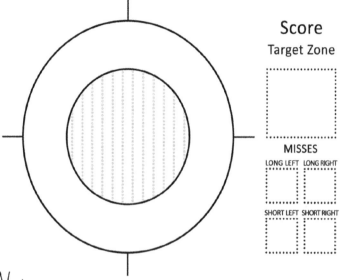

Score
Target Zone

MISSES
LONG LEFT   LONG RIGHT

SHORT LEFT   SHORT RIGHT

Notes

_____
_____
_____
_____
_____
_____
_____
_____

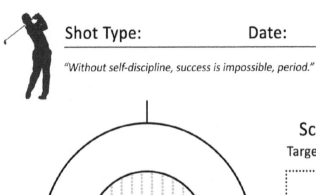

Shot Type: _____ Date: _____

"Without self-discipline, success is impossible, period."
— Lou Holtz

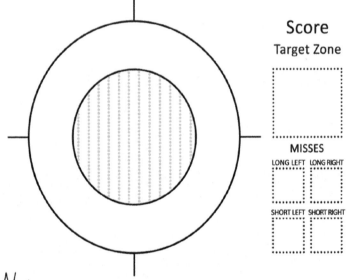

Score
Target Zone

MISSES
LONG LEFT LONG RIGHT

SHORT LEFT SHORT RIGHT

Notes

_____
_____
_____
_____
_____
_____
_____
_____

Shot Type: _____ Date: _____

"The will to win is important, but the will to prepare is vital."
— Joe Paterno

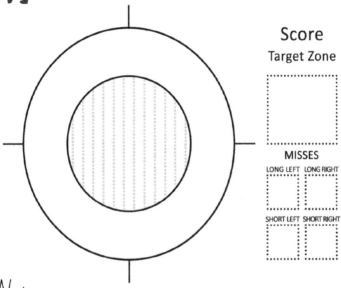

Score
Target Zone

MISSES
LONG LEFT   LONG RIGHT

SHORT LEFT SHORT RIGHT

Notes

_____

_____

_____

_____

_____

_____

_____

_____

_____

Shot Type: _____   Date: _____

"Strength does not come from winning. Your struggles develop your strengths. When you go through hardships and decide not to surrender, that is strength."
— Arnold Schwarzenegger

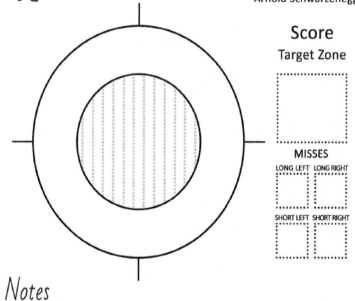

Score
Target Zone

MISSES
LONG LEFT   LONG RIGHT

SHORT LEFT   SHORT RIGHT

Notes

_____
_____
_____
_____
_____
_____
_____
_____

Shot Type: _____ Date: _____

"If you fail to prepare, you're prepared to fail."

– Mark Spitz

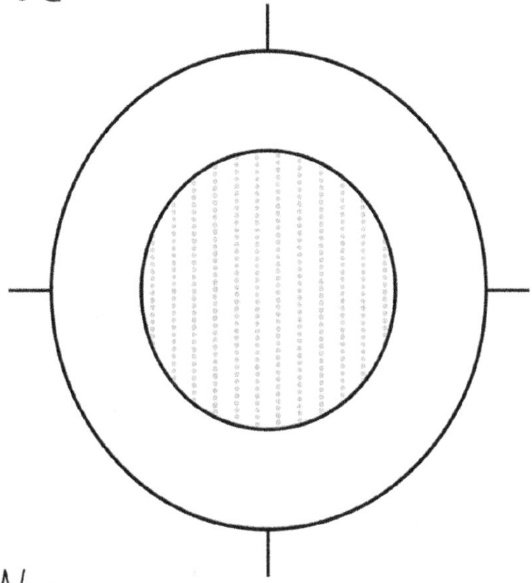

Score
Target Zone

MISSES
LONG LEFT LONG RIGHT

SHORT LEFT SHORT RIGHT

Notes

_____
_____
_____
_____
_____
_____
_____
_____
_____

Shot Type: _____   **Date:** _____

"Obstacles don't have to stop you. If you run into a wall, don't turn around and give up. Figure out how to climb it, go through it, or work around it."

– Michael Jordan

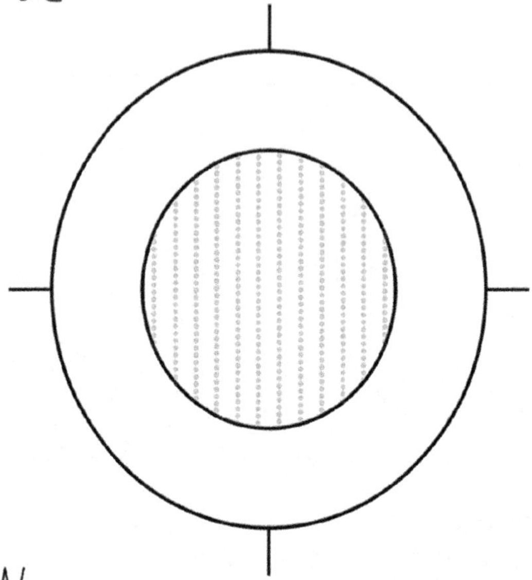

Score
Target Zone

MISSES
LONG LEFT   LONG RIGHT

SHORT LEFT   SHORT RIGHT

Notes

_____
_____
_____
_____
_____
_____
_____
_____
_____

Shot Type: _____ Date: _____

"Win if you can, lose if you must, but NEVER QUIT!"
— Cameron Trammell

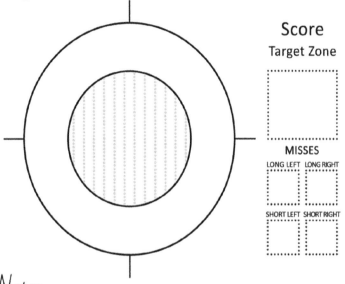

Score
Target Zone

MISSES
LONG LEFT LONG RIGHT

SHORT LEFT SHORT RIGHT

Notes

_____
_____
_____
_____
_____
_____
_____
_____
_____

Shot Type: _____   **Date:** _____

"You can't put a limit on anything. The more you dream, the farther you get."

– Michael Phelps

Score
Target Zone

MISSES
LONG LEFT   LONG RIGHT

SHORT LEFT   SHORT RIGHT

Notes

_____
_____
_____
_____
_____
_____
_____
_____

IDEAS/NOTES/THOUGHTS

"The world is full of magical things patiently waiting for our wits to grow sharper."
W.B. YEATS

The 11 Practice Principles
for Peak Performance

In episode 12 of Making A Club Champion. Dave Alred was featured on the podcast.

Dave Alred is one of the best coaches in the world today. Boasting clients including Jonny Wilkinson, Luke Donald, Padraig Harrington and Francesco Molinari.

Dave Alred, has an innate ability to help athletes exceed their own expectations. Gaining a Ph.D. in Performing Under Pressure from Loughborough University and over 30 years of experience in the field of performance psychology.

The below is deconstructed cliff notes from the episode to use as a guide when lost, stuck or lacking structure to your practice.

1. Confidence is based on fact

"If you're going to practice you need to practice against numbers, otherwise how do you know if you are getting any better? So whether it is nearer to the pin or consistency, there will be numbers to show it. And the biggest thing about confidence is; Confidence should be based on fact i.e. you have already done it before.

You look like a pretty good golfer to me, doesn't mean diddly squat frankly. But if you know, you can hit 10 shots with a 54-degree wedge and 5 of those will be within 10ft of the pin and the others will be within 15ft of the pin. Now that is a fact. You have achieved that. How can I get that even better? I can get more shots within 10ft and so on...

Keep track of all of your previous practice data, and try to beat your previous best. You now have facts that you can actually prove that you can do it: and therefore for when you went into a tournament, there was a factual basis behind your approach and it gave you a lot more confidence."

2. Behavior

"I won't actually tell players when they are doing something wrong. I will tell them when they are doing something right. If you draw attention to a behavior you do not want to repeat, the chance is you will only get more of it. But if you draw attention to behavior you want to repeat, hopefully, you will get more of that.

3. Practice

"Everyday there should be a component that puts you under the pump. Otherwise, the behavior you get to exhibit is not related to the tournament, so there Is no point in doing it."

4. Affirmations

"We certainly do not like writing about ourselves positively but yet that self of scan ticket is a really big competent whether or not you are confident. It's not something you keep and put on a tee shirt, but it is something you write about yourself and you put it inside your scorecard.

It is not necessarily I am a good guy and I will be number one in the world. But you could be one of the best in the world providing I play my own game."

An example of an affirmation: "Tall in execution and singularly ruthless in mind. Feeling excited/nervous, maybe uncomfortable—it's great—it's your field for a great performance—a BIG performance."

5. Self-talk

"I would be worried if a golfer was asking himself questions I would rather have the self-talk be like; I have a PW here, and I know statistically that I should be able to put 50% of these within 9ft of the in of the pin. I need to look where the pin placement is, is there 9ft ft all around the pin and if there is I should be able to go for it. So I would rather have dialogue like that which is related to their training and their margins rather than questions."

6. Personal Qualities

"Humility and toughness, those two do not necessarily go together. You get people who are humble, but not very strong. So you have to work on that area. And then you get people who are very strong-willed but lean towards arrogance and they are not willing to learn and not do anything different.

I remind the players I work with. Humility Is, I do not know all the answers, and I can still improve no matter how good I am now. This is the attitude. And the toughness is when things get difficult—I still keep going. If you get those two things together, you have a pretty potent combination. For someone to do something quite special."

7. Comfort

"All the golfers I work with, I try and get them to create a behavior match, in other words, to be almost playing the tournament before we get onto the first tee. One of the things I do now to make the preparation (or the warm-up) is to have quite a bit of unpredictability about it. So the brain doesn't get comfortable.

If the brain is comfortable and something doesn't quite match your intention on the first tee. Then it can really throw you. But if the brain is really on edge and expecting things and able to deal with them. Then you are in a much better position to cope with whatever happens."

8. Attitude

"Wherever you are and whoever you are, you can always get better. But that doesn't imply that there's fault with what you are doing at the moment. It's never ever too late."

9. Productivity

"I make a list and start knocking things off the list. I will make a list of the things I need to do. Set a kitchen timer for 45 minutes and go absolutely bananas. And when the bell goes, I will see how much I have done, and often I will just keep on going."

10. Goal Setting

"I don't set goals. I set myself tasks and process goals. The things that I can control, I do take on board and set myself targets and processes that I want to achieve. For example, just lately I have been training and even if I don't feel like I still make myself do it, so I get very disciplined. And It feels like I am in a good position to demand discipline of others who I work with."

11. Accountability Action Challenge

" Go through a week and write down three good things that have happened each day. And when you get to the Sunday. Sit down read all those that you have written and say why am I better than I was last Monday? If I keep my mind open, I can improve. I can be in a better place by next week., by virtue of how I approach this week.

Dave Alred: Episode 12, MakingAClubChampion.com

Golf Performance Journals

Also by

Making A Club Champion

Golf Data: Performance Statics About Your Game.

Short Game: Master Your Wedge game

Long Game: 290 Yards & In Driving range Journal

College Golf Journal: Productivity & Performance Planner

For more information visit:

MakingAClubChampion.com

CHRIS BAKER; broke par at age 13 and won his first, Men's Club Championship at age 15.

He went onto represent Great Britain and Ireland on the Swifts Tour competing in America. And was a winner on the Faldo Series.

Gaining a scholarship to America at University of Charlotte, North Carolina. He won two NCAA Conference Championships with his team.

He has won a combination of three Men's Club Championship's. And was part of the winning team at the Halford Hewitt in 2010, the biggest amateur tournament in the world.

The host of the show, 'Making A Club Champion.' Chris has always been interested in how the best coaches and players in the world of golf spend their time practicing and how to make that as effective as possible.

Chris has caddied multiple times on the European Tour at the dreaded final stage qualifying school.

He gained a strength and conditioning qualification in San Francisco and experiments in performance-based nutrition, competing in Ironman triathlons entirely on cashew butter, coconut oil, and medium chain triglycerides.

Chris is also an avid collector of Banksy artwork. He lives in Bristol, United Kingdom.

Made in the USA
Las Vegas, NV
03 February 2021